In their Early Twenties

A STUDY OF GLASGOW YOUTH

BY

T. FERGUSON

Professor of Public Health, University of Glasgow

AND

J. CUNNISON

*Formerly Director of Social and Economic Research
University of Glasgow*

Published for

THE NUFFIELD FOUNDATION

BY THE

OXFORD UNIVERSITY PRESS

LONDON NEW YORK TORONTO

1956

Oxford University Press, Amen House, London E.C.4

GLASGOW NEW YORK TORONTO MELBOURNE WELLINGTON
BOMBAY CALCUTTA MADRAS KARACHI
CAPE TOWN IBADAN NAIROBI ACCRA SINGAPORE

———

PRINTED IN GREAT BRITAIN

PREFACE

IN 1951 we published an account of some of the adventures that befell 1,349 Glasgow lads during the first 3 years after they left school in January 1947. This group included all who left schools in the city at the earliest permitted age, then 14 years. The end of that earlier study left these lads, at the age of 17, in very varying states. Some, usually those who had started with the advantage of a good home, were already firmly embarked on an apprenticeship or period of training that seemed likely to lead to skilled employment; some were still in uneasy passage from one casual stop-gap job to another; a few were already apparently bent on following a career of crime. The future of many obviously still hung in the balance.

This present study is a natural sequel to our earlier work. For those of the original group of lads who fell into one or other of two categories—those who embarked on National Service on attaining the age of 18 years and those who, rejected as medically unfit for Service, remained in civil life—this present study carries the story on for 5 more years, to the time when they were 22 years of age. All the information gathered in the course of the earlier study was, of course, available for the present work.

Inevitably there has arisen in recent years a great deal of speculation, not always very firmly founded, about the effects of National Service on the careers of young men. Much of the material in this report touches that question, but it is not easy to present material of the kind fairly and objectively in a way that would permit direct comparison between those who had been on Service and those who had not. The issues are too complicated for that; the yardsticks available for making the necessary measurements are not always all that might be desired and, in practice, it is difficult to obtain a series of lads whose performance can fairly be compared with that of those who had been away on Service.

Even apart from the effects of National Service, we have been struck by the extent of the drift away from trade skill which marked the careers of these lads between the ages of 17 and 22, and by the great importance of earlier background in moulding subsequent career.

It would not have been possible to carry through this study without the devoted help of the group of experienced social workers who voluntarily gave so much of their time to visiting the lads at regular intervals to keep accurate records of their performance. We are also greatly indebted to the Service authorities concerned, and especially to the Medical Departments of the Royal Navy, the Army, and the Royal Air Force, and to Mr. S. Rosenbaum of the Army Medical Statistical Branch, for co-operation which made it possible to relate some aspects of the Service experience of those lads who undertook National Service to their performance before and after they had been away. The Chief Constable of Glasgow kindly enabled us to study the criminal records of lads included in our survey. The lads themselves co-operated with us to an extent much greater than might have been expected: their co-operation is a fitting tribute to the sympathetic understanding and common sense of the social workers who kept in touch with them.

We very gladly acknowledge the help which we have received in the preparation of this report from Miss Duff and Miss Hatrick, of the University Departments of Public Health and Social Research; and the solicitude of Mr. Allen Sanderson, of the staff of the Nuffield Foundation, in seeing the work through the press.

T. F.

J. C.

CONTENTS

I
Background

1

In 1936 the Carnegie United Kingdom Trustees appointed three special officers who, each in his own area, should spend some years in an intensive study of the situation and experience of young men between the ages of 18 and 25, especially those who were unemployed. This field-work was carried out between 1936 and 1939, partly in Glasgow, partly in Liverpool, and partly in South Wales; and the findings were described in a report, *Disinherited Youth*,[1] published in 1943. That report, concerned chiefly with the experience of young unemployed men between the ages of 18 and 23 in the depressed days of the 1930s, disclosed that the amount of unrest, disappointment, and social misery among the young folk covered by the survey was very great. The investigators found that many of the causes producing the prevalent misery had their roots far back in the social conditions of the young folk's earlier upbringing: the authors of the report were driven to conclude that much of the damage had already been done 'during those very important and impressionable 4 years' between the ages of 14 and 18.

2

That earlier survey, with its clear recognition of the importance of the immediate post-school years in shaping the subsequent careers of young people, was one of the factors which moved us to carry out in Glasgow a study, of which the results were published in 1951 under the title *The Young Wage-Earner*.[2] Our study was based on, and included, all the boys—1,349 in number—who left school at the age of 14 years, then the earliest permitted age, on one of the prescribed school-leaving dates, of which there are in Glasgow four in the course

---

[1] *Disinherited Youth: A Survey 1936–39*, edited by C. Cameron, Carnegie United Kingdom Trust, Edinburgh, Constable, 1943.

[2] *The Young Wage-Earner*, T. Ferguson and J. Cunnison. Published for The Nuffield Foundation by the Oxford University Press, 1951.

of each year. The date chosen was 26 January 1947. It is not easy to obtain a sample which will afford an accurate cross-section of the youth of a great city. For example, it was estimated that at that time about one-quarter of the school population elected to continue at school beyond the earliest school-leaving date; and a wide variety of circumstances may help to determine whether a lad leaves school at the earliest permitted age or goes on to further education. As was pointed out in *The Young Wage-Earner*, some of these reasons are economic, as where the child is one of a large family, or where the father is dead, or where some other family circumstance makes it necessary for the young person to begin to earn at the earliest possible moment. Sometimes the parents consider that a child is not bright and feel that there is little to be gained by his continued attendance at school. Sometimes the young person himself has no inclination to continue, especially if he has set his mind on a particular kind of work for which he imagines further schooling to be of little service. Again, children who, by reason of physical or mental handicap, are being educated in special schools commonly continue at school beyond the earliest permitted leaving age; and there is the further group, of widely varying ages, receiving education and training in approved schools, many of whom are not allowed to leave at the ordinary school-leaving age.

A great deal of information was collected about the 1,349 boys included in the study: about their school life—their health while at school, their attendance-record, their scholastic attainment, their physical condition, their temperamental qualities, and their job-preference on leaving school; about their home background, their family circumstances, and difficulties; and, by 6-monthly home visitation during the 3 years after they left school, about their performance when they went out into the industrial world—how they fared in relation to health, to employment and unemployment, to apprenticeship or training, and to use of leisure. The survey covered the period from January 1947 to January 1950, by which time all the lads had passed their 17th birthday.

At the end of the 3 years' study, 75 out of every 100 boys were in manual work and 25 in non-manual. Ignoring that distinction, very nearly 50 per cent. were on the way to a skilled trade or profession, roughly 25 per cent. in medium grades of work, and roughly 25 per cent. in unskilled labour or dead-end jobs. High occupational status at the end of the survey was directly associated with certain characteristics shown throughout the period—constancy to employers and jobs; a sense of purpose when changes were made; consistently keen interest in the job; good use of leisure; and little loss of working time through unemployment. Overall, 74 per cent. of the boys considered that, in the job they held at age 17, they had reached the kind of work in which they intended to remain permanently: 26 per cent. still considered their latest job as merely a stop-gap. Three out of every four of the boys had never made use of the most obvious facilities for continued education—evening continuation classes—and about half had never had a church connexion or joined any organized social group. One hundred and fifty-six of the boys, 11·6 per cent. of the total, had been convicted on 237 occasions between their 8th and 17th birthdays; 103 were convicted on one occasion only, 53 had convictions ranging in number from two to seven, the great majority of the convictions being for theft or attempted theft.

The showing of the boys, when freed from school discipline, was heavily coloured by their earlier social environment. The conditions bearing on the character and performance of youth are always a mixture of the old and the new; there is the influence of conditions persisting from the past which put these lads to grow up in the city, mainly in tenements of the older type, condemning a substantial minority to pass their boyhood in the slums, very often exposed to the evils of serious overcrowding in the home. On the other hand, there are the influences of more recent date—the improvement in material conditions effected by the growth of public services, particularly rehousing, the operation of the policy of full employment and the steadier household income which results from it, advice and guidance in finding suitable work, and the multiplication of means for the better use of leisure.

3

It has been considered desirable to refer in some detail to this study of immediate post-school years because the lads concerned in the work about to be described were drawn from those included in the earlier survey, so that a great deal of information was available about them and could be related to subsequent findings—an important point, for it became abundantly clear, as the Carnegie surveyors had previously found, that the events of the immediate post-school years profoundly influenced those which followed, just as they were themselves profoundly influenced by the circumstances of childhood. The present study is concerned with the experience of two groups of young men over a period of 2 years, while they were between the ages of 20 and 22—well within the age-band covered by the pre-war Carnegie survey. But circumstances have greatly changed during the past 20 years; two changes, in particular, are certain to have affected decisively the experience of the young men exposed to them. The unemployment and industrial depression of the 1930s have been replaced by a much better prospect of employment, even on Clydeside, where unemployment is still heavier than in most parts of England. For young people leaving school there is now no scarcity of jobs, though it is not always easy for a lad to obtain quickly the kind of job which he desires, with the result that many, tempted by high initial wages, find their way into unsuitable and dead-end jobs. It is much more difficult for a lad to obtain a job after he has passed his 17th birthday, partly because there are many jobs that are habitually filled by young post-school labour and normally keep boys in employment for only 2 years, and partly because many employers are reluctant to start new workers approaching their 18th birthday, with the imminent break of continuity of work—and subsequent reinstatement rights—involved in National Service. How lads in the 20–22 age-group fared in the matter of employment will emerge from the present study.

The other major change affecting the lives of young men is, of course, the introduction of compulsory National Service itself. It is obvious that any such fundamental change must have potential far-reaching effects. Adolescence is essentially a period of instability; and it is possible to regard the period of National Service as just another factor likely to interfere with the shaping of a lad's career, another disruptive influence; or, on the other hand, as a period of stability and discipline which may play an important part in moulding his character. Speaking at a conference held in Edinburgh in 1954 under the auspices of the British Association for Commercial and Industrial Education to discuss industry and National Service,[1] Dr. H. T. L. Robbie, Headmaster of Daniel Stewart's College, Edinburgh, said that he thought the average Scottish boy and his parents looked upon National Service as a break and an opportunity to come back to something different; but the boys of better quality almost entirely regarded it as a gap, with the result that they tended to leave school earlier than usual. It is not surprising that there has been much lively controversy about the effects of National Service. Some firms have reported that they found it to have little effect on the subsequent careers of their apprentices; others again, particularly in the Scottish industrial belt, have told us that many of their young trainees do not return to them after Service and that those who do return are often unsettled and poorer workers than before they went away. The General Council of the National Farmers' Union of Scotland, lamenting the movement of workers away from agriculture, has reported that 50 per cent. of the farm workers called up for National Service do not return to the industry.[2] At the Edinburgh conference mentioned above there was inevitably considerable difference of opinion among the educationists, industrialists, and Service personnel present on the effects of National Service upon young people.

4

The lads included in our present study fall into two groups —one containing 346 who had completed their period of National Service, the other containing 222 who had been rejected on medical grounds as unfit for Service and who had, therefore, remained in civil life. Of the 346 who had been on Service, 315 had served for the normal period of 2 years: 30 of the remaining 31 had served for shorter periods and had usually been discharged from Service on medical grounds; one had served for longer than the compulsory 2 years. The length of service in these 31 cases ranged from a few days upwards, and since the problems confronting these lads were different from those facing the others, their records have been excluded from

---

[1] *Scotsman*, 7 Oct. 1954.   [2] *Ibid.*, 25 Mar. 1955.

the body of this report, except where otherwise stated, and are
dealt with briefly in an appendix.

5

It is surprising that there has not been more effort to try to
estimate, by systematic controlled observation, the impact of
National Service on our young people, for the question must
surely rank as one of the major social issues of the day. Doubtless, scarcity of studies of this kind stems from the very considerable practical difficulties of interpretation, for it is not easy to
get two series of lads of similar age and social background, one
having done National Service, the other not, but otherwise
sufficiently comparable to permit balanced assessment of their
subsequent performance. The series are certain to differ substantially in physical condition and impairment, and may well
present other important differences—as, for example, in
scholastic ability or occupational status—which have to be
taken into account before the groups can be compared. Such
differences were encountered among the lads on whom this
study is based; but fortunately, from the vast amount of information available about their previous social and environmental history, and their performance in industry between the
ages of 14 and 17, it was possible to make some broad comparisons between the two groups. Even so, caution is necessary
in the interpretation of the results. It is to be remembered that
all the boys included in the original survey, from whom those
in the present study are drawn, had left school at the earliest
permitted age and were therefore probably drawn from less
privileged sections of the community; further, that young
people undergoing training or apprenticeship can apply for
deferment of National Service until they have completed their
period of training, and the majority in fact do so. It may well
be that the apprentices who elect to interrupt their apprenticeship at the age of 18 to undertake National Service are not
typical of the generality of apprentices; they may include more
than a fair share of those who are unsettled or who, for one
reason or another, are not getting on very well in their work.
The apprentices in this study who elected to go on Service at
the age of 18, for instance, included a larger proportion of
those drawn from lower strata of scholastic ability than did the

series of boys in the original survey who were serving apprenticeships at the age of 17, so that care is necessary in assessing
their performance subsequent to Service.

But even with all the difficulties and potential sources of
error involved, it has seemed to be worth while to record the
experience of those two groups of lads, if only because nowadays
we are none too well off for information about the lives of young
people in their early twenties. It may be that their experience
will serve to throw into relief some of the circumstances that
follow return from National Service; it may be that it will serve
to emphasize anew the fundamental importance of a good home
and a healthy social environment.

2

The Groups Studied

I

The present situation of lads included in the previous study

AT the end of *The Young Wage-Earner* study, early in 1950, the lads whom it embraced had only recently passed their 17th birthday and were still the better part of a year from the time when they would have to register under the National Service Acts. When, towards the end of 1952, nearly 3 years later, it was decided to embark upon this present study, it was realized that there might often be difficulty in re-establishing the happy relationships with the boys which had marked the earlier venture. Many changes in outlook and attitude take place between the ages of 17 and 20; and, in addition to the ordinary changes of growing up, there was the major complication of National Service.

It was necessary, as a first step, to find out which of the lads included in *The Young Wage-Earner* study had been called up for Service, which had been rejected as unfit for Service, and which deferred to enable them to complete a period of apprenticeship or other vocational training. It was known that a number of the 1,314 boys who were still included in the earlier study at its close had already left Glasgow before their 17th birthday: it had been possible to keep them under observation until the end of the study only through the kind co-operation of social agencies in different parts of the country. As a preliminary to the new approach all such were deleted from the list, as well as a few who had been tending to become un-co-operative before the end of the previous study. The names of the others were sent to the Regional Controller of the Ministry of Labour and National Service (who had been interested in the earlier study) with the request that he would be good enough to let us know, from his departmental records, which of the lads had been called up for National Service, which deferred, and which rejected as unfit for Service. For a variety of reasons it was found difficult to trace some of the young people even on the official files; but in the end it was possible to obtain accurate information about 1,115 of the lads concerning whom an extensive range of information was available from the earlier study. Of the 1,115

454 (40·7 per cent.) had been called up for National Service;

332 (29·8 per cent.) had been deferred to enable them to complete an apprenticeship or period of training;

253 (22·7 per cent.) had been rejected on medical grounds as unfit for National Service—73 being placed in grade III and 180 in grade IV;

66 (5·9 per cent.) had volunteered for Service before being called up; and

10 (0·9 per cent.) were working in the Merchant Navy or in coal-mines.

2

The groups selected

It was decided to confine this present investigation to the first and third of these groups—those who had actually reported for Service on, or within a few months after, reaching the age of 18 years, and those rejected on medical grounds as unfit for National Service. It would have been interesting to include also those whose Service had been deferred to enable them to complete their apprenticeships, in order to see to what extent, for instance, they returned to the jobs for which they had been trained when they came back to civil life after completing National Service; but that would have involved a long and protracted study, for many of these deferred apprentices could not complete National Service before they were 24 years of age and would not have been available for a study along the lines proposed until about 1958. By that time all sorts of complicating factors would have made it well-nigh impossible to set their experience against that of comparable groups. Indeed, it was realized very clearly from the outset that serious difficulties would beset any attempt to compare the performance over a period of years even of the two groups which it was intended to study; many of these difficulties will emerge in the course of this work.

3

Number of young men available for study

In practice we were able to include in the study only 346 of the 454 men who had been called up for National Service (76 per cent.) and only 222 of the 253 rejected as unfit for Service (87 per cent.). Not all the 108 Servicemen who were not included in the study were in fact available for study: some, for example, had been called up a little later than the others, and to have waited to complete a period of observation of them after discharge would have dragged out the investigation; some had extended their period of Service in the Forces. Of those who did return to civil life at the end of 2 years some never settled in Glasgow at all after discharge and some remained in the city for only a very short time before moving elsewhere. A few were left out because they did not wish to co-operate in the study, but they were far fewer than might have been expected, doubtless because the boys were already well aware of the implications of the method of continued observation which the study involved, having participated in the earlier one, and already being, in many cases, on friendly terms with the social worker who was to be visiting them in their own homes during the 2 years of this further study. It was possible to include in the study a relatively larger proportion of those who had been rejected as unfit, chiefly because they had not dispersed to such an extent as the lads who had been away on Service. We believe that the two groups of men included in the study can be regarded as reasonably typical of their fellows.

4

Previous background

In any consideration of what happened to these young men over a period of 2 critical years it is essential to keep ever in mind the background from which they were drawn. In the main they came from less privileged strata of society, often from the poorer, more overcrowded tenements of a great city. Nearly all were born about the end of 1932; 'cradled, therefore, in the lean years of the early 'thirties, years when the shadow of unemployment lay heavily over Clydeside, and nurtured largely during the war of 1939–45, years of storm and disorganization'. Those with whom we are now more immediately concerned represent but a fraction of the larger series whose adventures between the ages of 14 and 17 have already been described in *The Young Wage-Earner*, and they probably had, on the average, a poorer start in life than the original larger series.

One of the groups in this present study consisted of 222 men who had been medically rejected as unfit for National Service; to the troubles of a poor environment many of these men would add the restraints of illness or the aftermath of illness, some measure of physical incapacity which might or might not be a serious handicap in their everyday lives, and also, in many cases, some measure of the educational disadvantage that so often comes of prolonged illness in childhood and so often aggravates the difficulties of those whose struggle is already sufficiently hard.

The other group consisted of 346 men of similar age who had completed their National Service and returned to civil life. Most of the men in this second group had not had the advantages of learning a skilled trade, and such of them as had embarked upon an apprenticeship or period of training—just over one hundred in all—had chosen to interrupt that training to undertake their National Service instead of applying for deferment of Service until they had completed their training, as they were entitled to do. Although other motives doubtless played a part, it is probably a fair inference that many who interrupted their training in this way did so because they were not getting on very well in their apprenticeship; so that this group of lads who returned to civil life after Service may probably have been of less stable background than the average National Serviceman, though perhaps typical enough of the many who embarked upon their National Service at the age of 18. In later chapters we shall compare their achievements with those of the lads who were rejected as unfit for National Service. Together these two groups are probably sufficiently representative of many of the young people in our cities today; and if indeed they encounter more than their share of difficulties, that is all the more reason why we should study their experience.

5

School performance

Consider, first, the young men included in these two groups as they appeared as lads about to leave school in January 1947. At that time those destined to be rejected as unfit for National Service did not differ greatly in height from the other boys who left school at the earliest permitted moment; the group had more than its share of badly undersized youngsters, but by way of compensation it had also more than its share of taller boys. The average height of the group of lads who later went on National Service soon after their 18th birthday was rather above average, chiefly because it had less than its quota of badly undersized boys.

All the Glasgow boys included in *The Young Wage-Earner* study were medically examined when they were about to leave school in January 1947 by an experienced doctor attached to the school health service; they were placed by the doctor in one of three groups, 'A', 'B', or 'C', according to their physical condition. Nearly one-third of the boys who left school at that time were placed in category 'A', the best; and nearly one-third of the boys who later went on National Service at the age of 18 were similarly placed in category 'A'. The boys subsequently rejected as unfit for National Service fared worse: just over one-quarter of them were placed in category 'A' and the proportion in category 'C', at the bad end of the scale, was half as high again as in the whole group of boys leaving school at that time.

Similarly, the personality of the boys was assessed by their head teachers when they were about to leave school; the boys who subsequently went on Service at the age of 18 came out very much about the level of all 14-year-old school-leavers, but those who were subsequently rejected as unfit for Service showed a higher proportion at the poor end of the scale.

At school leaving, too, the boys were placed by their teachers in one of five groups, 'A', 'B', 'C', 'D', or 'E', according to general scholastic ability; here again the boys who went on Service at the age of 18 came very close to the general level of all the boys of their age who left school at that time, but the boys later rejected as unfit for National Service were of much poorer educational calibre: the proportion of them reaching categories 'A' or 'B', for instance, was less than half the overall figure, and there were half as many again in categories 'E' or 'D', at the poorer end of the scale. Thus, in all these assessments, made independently when the boys were about to leave school at the age of 14, the boys who embarked on Service at, or very soon after, their 18th birthday, had approximated reasonably closely to the average performance of school-leavers of their age, but the boys rejected as unfit for National Service cut altogether poorer figures.

6

Home circumstances

Similar comparisons can be made between these two groups of boys, and between them and school-leavers generally, in relation to home background. There was little to choose between the three series in the general quality of the home, as assessed by an experienced social worker when the boys left school; but, on comparing the types of housing districts in which the boys were living at that time, it was found that while the boys who subsequently embarked on National Service at the age of 18 were living in housing districts very similar in quality to the general pattern prevailing among 14-year-old school-leavers in the city as a whole, the lads rejected as unfit for National Service came from poorer housing districts; the proportion living in 'residential' or 'good working-class' areas, for instance, was little more than half the figure for all school-leavers and the proportion living in 'slum' areas half as high again.

In point of severity of overcrowding in the home there was little to choose between the general average figure—over 32 per cent. of lads were living in homes with three or more persons to each room—and the corresponding figure for lads rejected as unfit for National Service—31 per cent. The lads who went on Service at the age of 18 actually fared worst in this respect, with over 35 per cent. living at the age of 14 under conditions of crowding in the home of three or more persons per room.

The group of those who were rejected as unfit for National Service included less than a due proportion of lads whose fathers were skilled artisans and an excess of lads who were sons of unskilled manual labourers: the group of boys who went on National Service at the age of 18, on the other hand, had rather more than their quota of sons of skilled fathers, though they had also a rather higher than usual quota of sons of unskilled labourers. The proportion of boys whose father was already dead when they left school at the age of 14 was fully 10 per cent. for the entire group of lads who left school at that age, rather less among the boys subsequently rejected for National Service, and considerably less among those who embarked on Service at the age of 18.

Considered in relation to these indexes of home background, then, the differences between the groups are perhaps less decisive than those arising from assessments of school performance; but it is worthy of note that in some respects—such as the kind of housing district in which they lived and the occupational groups to which their fathers belonged—the boys rejected for National Service hailed from a poorer social background than the boys who went on Service at the age of 18 or the generality of boys of their age who left school at the earliest permitted moment.

7

Nature of employment

Just before they left school at the age of 14, all the boys included in *The Young Wage-Earner* study were asked what kind of job they desired to take up. One in every five had no preference at that time, but more than half of the boys (56 per cent.) wanted skilled manual work. Among the group who went on National Service at the age of 18, the proportion who had wished skilled manual work was just short of that figure; but among the boys rejected as unfit for Service it was appreciably lower.

At the end of that study, when the boys in the parent investigation were 17 years of age, some 47 per cent. of them were serving an apprenticeship or period of training, 4 per cent. had already fallen through an apprenticeship on which they had embarked, 18 per cent. were in semi-skilled manual work, about 25 per cent. were in non-manual jobs, mostly in offices or in the distributive trades, some of these jobs having only poor prospects; and the balance were in unskilled work.

At the age of 17 three out of every four of the boys were

prepared to accept the jobs in which they then found themselves as the kind of work in which they would continue: the others still regarded their jobs as merely stop-gap.

Among the boys who subsequently embarked on National Service at the age of 18, about one-third were serving an apprenticeship at the age of 17, the proportion who had already lapsed from an apprenticeship was nearly twice as high as normal, and the proportion of lads who were unskilled manual labourers was higher than the usual figure among boys of that age. The proportion of boys who were prepared to accept the kind of job in which they were employed at the age of 17 as their life's work was smaller than might have been expected. Among those rejected as unfit for National Service the position was even worse. Just over one in four of those lads was serving an apprenticeship and nearly 40 per cent. were unskilled manual labourers: one in every three still felt dissatisfied with the job in which he found himself at the age of 17, regarding it as merely stop-gap.

8

Working time lost and frequency of change of job

There were also differences between the groups in the amount of working time which the boys had lost (from all causes) during the 3 years between their 14th and 17th birthdays. In the parent series, 40 per cent. of the lads lost no time during these 3 years, but one in every six lost 3 months or more. Among those who went on Service at 18 the working time lost between the ages of 14 and 17 was less than the overall figure; but among those rejected as unfit for National Service it was considerably higher—less than one in three had lost no time and about one in four had been off work for 3 months or more in the course of the 3 years.

Inevitably, in the ordinary course of shaping a career, there had been a good deal of change of jobs in the 3 post-school years; of the boys who left Glasgow schools in January 1947 on attaining the age of 14, two in every three changed jobs on one or two occasions in the course of the 3 years. But a small minority of the lads kept changing with a frequency that suggested that there was something unsettled about them or something undesirable about the kinds of job they were getting; thus, of all the boys who left school at that time, 9 per cent. changed jobs on four or more occasions between the ages of 14 and 17. By comparison, over 16 per cent. of those who went on National Service at the age of 18 had changed jobs on four or more occasions between the ages of 14 and 17, while in the group rejected as unfit for National Service the proportion who had changed jobs four or more times was even higher, over 17 per cent. It may well have been that the reasons for this repeated changing of jobs were different in the two series of cases.

9

Membership of organized social groups

At the age of 17 just over 40 per cent. of all the boys who had left Glasgow schools at the earliest opportunity in January 1947 were members of an organized social group—Boy Scouts, Boys' Brigade, youth clubs, and others. Among the lads who went on National Service at the age of 18 the proportion was very similar; but among those rejected as unfit for National Service the proportion who were members of youth organizations was only 33 per cent.

10

Previous history of called-up and rejected groups compared

Taking all these circumstances into account, and in spite of the lads' relatively poor showing in such things as the proportion who were unskilled labourers, the proportion who had already fallen through an apprenticeship on which they had embarked, and the excessively frequent change of job between the ages of 14 and 17—all factors rather suggestive of some measure of instability—it seems to be a reasonable inference that the boys who went on National Service at the age of 18 in the main approximated fairly closely to, or fell not much short of, the average level of performance of all the boys of their time who left city schools at the earliest permitted age. The boys rejected as unfit for National Service, on the other hand, had a much poorer record: they hailed from poorer districts, were of poorer quality in a range of assessments made at the time of leaving school, and had, between the ages of 14 and 17, returned a much poorer performance at work. These findings must clearly be kept in mind when comparing in this present study the performance, between the ages of 20 and 22, of the lads who went on Service at the age of 18 and of those who, rejected as unfit for National Service, remained in civil life. Apart from any influence, for good or ill, which the period of Service may have had on the subsequent careers of those called up, it would clearly be unrealistic, in view of their past record, to expect the rejected lads to do as well as those who went on Service, other things being equal.

Incidentally, since one of the groups with which we are immediately concerned, the lads who went on Service at 18, approximated to the average level of performance of all the boys who left city schools at the earliest permitted age, and since the other group fell far short of average standards, it is a reasonable assumption that the large group who were, in the nature of things, excluded from this study—those whose National Service was deferred to enable them to complete an apprenticeship— must have been in the main of substantially better quality than the groups now under review.

I I

Previous background of lads who served in the Army and Royal Air Force compared

Though the group of young men included in the study who completed their 2 years' Service in the Royal Air Force was comparatively small—68 as compared with 244 who served in the Army—it is possible to draw some broad comparisons from the previous records of the lads who went to these Services. At the time they left school, for instance, there was a much higher proportion of undersized boys among those who subsequently did their Service in the Army—some 40 per cent. were then under 57 inches in height as compared with only 24 per cent. of the boys who served in the Royal Air Force; the proportion placed in category 'C' (the worst) in point of physical and personality assessments was higher among those who served in the Army, and the difference in scholastic assessment was substantial: 32 per cent. of the boys who served in the Royal Air Force fell into categories 'D' or 'E' (the two lowest) compared with 46 per cent. of those who served in the Army.

Similarly, the boys who served in the Royal Air Force came from homes assessed as better by an experienced social worker; the proportion of slum-dwellers among them was much lower, and far fewer of them came from severely overcrowded homes; 23 per cent. of the Air Force lads lived in homes in which there were three or more persons per room, whereas the corresponding figure for those who served in the Army was 38 per cent. The proportion of boys who were the sons of fathers employed in skilled manual work was much the same in the two groups, but a higher proportion of the fathers of boys who served in the Army were unskilled manual labourers.

The proportion of lads who had wished to obtain skilled manual work when they left school was higher among those who served in the Royal Air Force, and although the proportion actually in process of serving apprenticeships at the age of 17 was slightly higher among the boys who did their Service in the Army, and the proportion who had already broken an apprenticeship on which they had embarked was also higher, the proportion who were unskilled manual labourers at 17 was more than twice as high among the lads who served in the Army as among those who served in the Royal Air Force. Working time lost (from all causes) between the ages of 14 and 17 was considerably greater among those who later served in the Army. The proportion of boys who were members of an organized social group at the age of 17 was higher among the lads who went to serve in the Royal Air Force than among those who went into the Army.

When all these things are taken into consideration, it is impossible to avoid the conclusion that the boys who undertook Service in the Royal Air Force had enjoyed at home considerable environmental advantages over those who served in the Army, and that their general standard of performance, both at school and at work, had been better; these, again, are obviously factors that have to be kept in mind when comparing the achievements of lads from the two Services after their return to civil life.

12

Ministry of Labour grouping of men who served in the Army related to height and weight at school leaving, and at entry to, and discharge from, the Army

We are informed by the Army authorities that of the boys in this study who did their National Service in the Army and for whom the relevant information is available, 68½ per cent. had been placed in grade I at the Ministry of Labour medical examination, 31 per cent. in grade II, and ½ per cent. in grade III. These proportions changed slightly on the boys' entry into the Army, owing to reassessment of their medical grades; in particular, some were discharged as grade IV. There is a probability that the proportions of grade II in our sample is higher and of grade I lower than those for the country as a whole, where the estimate from a recent sample shows about one in grade II to four in grade I. On the other hand, by the time the boys were released, the proportions in this Glasgow group were roughly the same as for the country as a whole—so that the Glasgow group had made a more than average improvement while on National Service.

The changes in height and weight between leaving school and entry into the Army are shown in Table 1.

TABLE 1

Average height and weight on leaving school and entering Army, and average gains between leaving school and entering Army: 218 National Servicemen for whom relevant information is available

Grade (Ministry of Labour examination)	Number of men	Average height on leaving school	Average height on entry into Army	Average gain (between leaving school and entry into Army)	Average weight on leaving school	Average weight on entry into Army	Average gain in weight (between leaving school and entering Army)
I . .	150	57·9″	66·4″	8·5″	88·1 lb.	132·5 lb.	44·4 lb.
II . .	67	56·7″	66·2″	9·6″	80·7 lb.	125·5 lb.	44·8 lb.
III . .	1	59·0″	64·0″	5·0″	96·0 lb.	128·0 lb.	32·0 lb.
	218	57·5″	66·4″	8·8″	85·9 lb.	130·4 lb.	44·5 lb.

The grade II men (as judged by the Ministry of Labour) were shorter on average when they left school than those placed in grade I, but on entering the Army this difference had almost disappeared. In weight, however, the grade II men were at a disadvantage on both occasions.

13

Men rejected on medical grounds as unfit for Service

If the 253 boys in the original study who were later rejected as unfit for National Service are related to the 520 who were accepted as fit and posted for Service (454 called up for National Service and 66 who volunteered before being called up), they would represent a rejection rate equal to about 33 per cent. of those examined. According to an article in the *Ministry of Labour Gazette*,[1] on the 'Call-up and Deferment of 1929–1936 Classes', for all age-classes taken together the unfit men represent approximately $17\frac{1}{2}$ per cent. of the total number medically examined. It may well be that national figures for 18-year-olds only would show a rather higher proportion of unfit men, because lads deferred will be excluded from the group. But the fact remains that the national figures for all ages obviously show a lower proportion of rejections than that experienced among the two groups of 18-year-old Glasgow boys embraced in this study.

We have not sought access to the official schedules of the results of these lads' medical examinations by the Recruiting Boards. But from our knowledge of their previous medical history, and from what they themselves have told us, it is not difficult to form a fairly accurate impression of the probable principal reasons for their rejection in some 85 per cent. of the boys classified as unfit. In 188 cases the cause of rejection appeared to be tolerably clear. Some of the lads were of very poor general physique, some were of very poor scholastic attainment. Forty-seven suffered from deafness, otorrhoea, or associated ear conditions; 21 from defective vision; 29 from lung conditions other than frank pulmonary tuberculosis; 17 from pulmonary tuberculosis, sometimes old, sometimes recently suspected as a result of mass radiographic examination; 6 from non-pulmonary tuberculosis or its results; 8 from alimentary disorders, including peptic ulcer; 8 from heart disease and 4 others from the effects of rheumatic fever; 8 from the results of old injuries; 7 from deformities of one kind or another, sometimes probably the result of old injuries; 6 from skin disorders; 4 from asthma; 4 from nephritis; 4 from varicose veins; 4 from foot disabilities; 3 from 'nervous debility'; and one each from disseminated sclerosis, osteomyelitis, poliomyelitis, hydrocele, fibrositis, and thymus abnormality; 2 were illiterate.

3

On National Service

1

The lads involved

ALTOGETHER 346 of the lads included in this study had been called up, or volunteered, for National Service at, or very soon after, the age of 18; 315 of them served for the ordinary period of 2 years and thereafter returned to civil life, one served for longer than 2 years, and 30 were discharged from Service before the completion of the 2-year period, chiefly on medical grounds. This chapter is concerned primarily with the 315 who served for 2 years and then returned to civil life; the 31 who served for periods other than this will be dealt with briefly in an appendix. Three of the 315 lads who completed 2 years' Service had been in the Royal Navy, 244 in the Army, and 68 in the Royal Air Force.

There are obviously two ways of obtaining information about how a lad fared on Service—one from the lad himself; the other from the Service authorities. It would scarcely be reasonable to expect the two points of view to correspond too closely. At the first visit in his own home after his return each Serviceman was asked about his Service experience and what he thought about Service life.

2

Service overseas

Two of the 3 sailors, 23 of the 68 airmen, and 172 of the 244 soldiers had served outside Britain—in all, 197 of the 315. Of the soldiers who served overseas, the largest group served in the Far East (including a few in Korea); the other main theatres were Germany and the Middle East.

3

Service duties

One hundred and forty-two of the men who served in the Army reported that, in the main, their work while on Service had been of a 'military' nature, 46 said they had been engaged chiefly in work of a 'trade' nature, while the remaining 56 regarded their duties as falling under 'other' headings. A relatively high proportion of the men who were in the Army seemed to have served in the R.A.O.C., and there is some indication that a lower proportion of those who had suffered least unemployment between the ages of 14 and 17 joined the R.A.O.C.; thus, 37 of the 63 men who served in the R.A.O.C. (59 per cent.) had experienced no unemployment between the ages of 14 and 17, while 73 per cent. of all the men who served in the Army had had no unemployment between these ages. Of the 68 men who had been in the Royal Air Force, 32 described their duties as predominantly 'military', 7 as chiefly of a 'trade' nature, and 29 as 'other'. Of the three who served in the Royal Navy, one classified his duties as predominantly 'military', one as 'trade', and one as 'other'.

Some of the Service jobs on which the men were employed seemed to contrast oddly with their civil occupations, which is not surprising; and the men themselves realized that this was inevitable. At the 1954 Edinburgh conference on industry and National Service, Brigadier F. G. A. Parsons, deputy director of manpower planning at the War Office, referring to the difficulty of fitting National Servicemen into the right trade and corps, said that each man's case was considered carefully and individually: 'The chief concern of discontent is the fact that we cannot train every man in the trade we want, because the Army is not all tradesmen. It is a fighting Service. Forty-two per cent. of our National Service intake goes to the R.A.C., the Royal Artillery, and the Infantry, and these corps have fewer trades in them which are equivalent to civilian trades.'[1]

In this series of 315 men, 55—8 in the Royal Air Force and 47 in the Army—reported that they had received some training in a trade while on Service, and 14 of these said that the Service training counted towards civilian apprenticeship.

4

Promotion on Service

Fifty-one of the 315 men reported that they had received promotion while on Service, 8 in the Royal Air Force and 43

[1] *Scotsman*, 7 Oct. 1954.

in the Army. Doubtless in some of these cases the promotion was of an 'acting' nature and perhaps of short duration, for not all of the 51 held non-commissioned rank at the time they left the Services. The men who reported that they had been promoted while on National Service were compared with the others in relation to their height at the time of leaving school; their personality and scholastic assessments, as made by the school authorities at that time; whether they were members of an organized social group at the age of 17; and the kind of work in which they had been employed at that age. A higher proportion of taller lads had received promotion: the average school-leaving height of the N.C.O.s was greater than that of the privates (or their equivalents). Thus, taking the Services together, of lads less than 59 inches in height when they left school at 14, 12 per cent. were promoted, as compared with 24 per cent. of those whose height was 59 inches or more.

Twenty-two per cent. of the lads who had been placed on leaving school in category 'A' (the best) in point of general personality-assessment reported that they had been promoted while on Service, as compared with 18 per cent. of those who had been placed in category 'B' (intermediate) and 15 per cent. of those placed in category 'C', the worst.

Five of the 36 boys (14 per cent.) placed in categories 'A' and 'B' (the best) in scholastic ability at the time of leaving school were promoted while on National Service; 30 of the 143 (21 per cent.) placed in category 'C' (intermediate) were promoted; and 16 of the 136 (12 per cent.) placed in categories 'D' and 'E', the poorest in scholastic ability.

There was no difference in the proportion of men promoted while on Service between those who had been members of some form of organized youth club at the age of 17 and those who had not been members of such an organization.

The highest proportion of men promoted during Service was found among those who had been engaged in semi-skilled manual work at the age of 17, 24 per cent. The proportion promoted was lower among those who had been serving apprenticeships to skilled manual trades (16 per cent.) and among those who had been engaged in non-manual work (18 per cent.); it was lowest among the men who had been unskilled manual labourers (11 per cent.).

5

Attitude of the men to National Service

One hundred and eighty-four (58·4 per cent.) of the men, asked on the occasion of the first visit to their homes how they had liked Service life, replied that they had quite enjoyed being on Service—2 of the 3 who served in the Royal Navy, 44 of the 68 who served in the Royal Air Force, and 138 of the 244 who served in the Army. Fifty-seven (18·1 per cent.) were quite certain that they had not enjoyed National Service—11 who served in the Royal Air Force and 46 who served in the Army. The remaining 74 (23·5 per cent.) had no strong views on the subject one way or the other. Since it seemed possible that this reaction to Service might have been unduly coloured by the recent proximity of the event, the men were asked the same question again 2 years later; the result showed comparatively little change, for on this occasion 59 per cent. replied that they had liked their period on Service, 27 per cent. said they had not enjoyed Service, and 14 per cent. were more or less neutral in their attitude to it, some of those who had been neutral 2 years previously apparently having made up their minds 'against' in the interval.

It is not surprising, therefore, that when asked whether they preferred Service or civilian life, the great majority of the returned ex-Servicemen expressed a preference for civilian life; the general attitude was that Service was just a job that had to be done. Twenty-one (6·7 per cent.), on the other hand, said they preferred Service life, while 7 were neutral on the subject.

Posting overseas did not appear to influence greatly the men's liking for Service life; of 23 airmen who served overseas, none preferred Service life, though one was neutral; neither of the 2 sailors who served overseas had a preference for Service life; 14 of the 172 soldiers who had been overseas preferred life in the Services: so that, taking all three Services together, 14 of the 197 who served overseas (7·1 per cent.) preferred Service life, a figure practically the same as that among men who did their Service in this country.

When liking for, or dislike of, Service life was compared with certain earlier social and environmental factors, it emerged that the proportion of men who liked or disliked Service life bore no special relationship either to the nature of their duties while on Service or to the kind of job in which they had been employed at the age of 17. Similarly, those who came from homes that had been assessed as 'good' when they left school disliked Service just as frequently as did those from indifferent homes. There was a tendency for the proportion of those who disliked Service to be higher among those of poor scholastic ability; and a relatively large proportion of those who disliked Service lived in 'new' local authority houses; relatively few lived in 'good' or 'fair' working-class houses of the older type.

TABLE 2

The attitude (at age 20) of returned National Servicemen to Service life, analysed in relation to level of scholastic attainment and type of housing district in which the lad lived when he left school: expressed as a percentage of men involved

Earlier background	Attitude to Service life		
	Liked	Disliked	Neutral
Scholastic assessment			
'A', 'B', or 'C' (good or fair) (179)* . .	60	16	24
'D' or 'E' (poor) (136)	56	21	23
Type of housing district			
'Good' or 'Fair' district of older type (141)	62	15	23
'Poor' or 'Slum' district of older type (88) .	58	17	25
'New' local-authority housing area (86) . .	53·5	24·5	22

* The figures in brackets in this and subsequent tables show the numbers 'at risk', i.e. those for whom the relevant information was available.

Twenty-one per cent. of the men reported that they had experienced difficulty in settling back into civil life after completing their National Service: the difficulties of these men are discussed further in Chapters 4 and 5.

6

Admission to Army medical units

The authorities of all three Services generously co-operated in this study by making available certain data from official records relative to the men included in it. In practice, it was not found to be very helpful to try to link up the kind of information on a Serviceman's discharge papers with his condition or performance in civil life before or soon after Service, but through the kindness of the War Office some interesting information has been placed at our disposal about the medical histories of the men while they were serving in the Army and on some points of relationship between these Army records and certain data already available about the medical histories of the lads before they went on Service.

TABLE 3

Distribution of admissions to Army medical units of 260 National Servicemen for whom relative information is available

No. of admissions	No. of men	Total stay (days)	Average days
0	145	..	..
1	73	1,256	17·2
2	27	879	16·5
3	9	305	11·3
4	3	296	24·7
5	1	200	40·0
6	2	217	18·1
	260	3,153	..

'Admission to medical unit' is defined as a stay of 48 hours or more. Since there is no 'home nursing' in the Army, the civilian equivalent to the figures quoted in Table 3 is more like 'absence from work on account of illness' than purely hospital treatment. The duration of stay in a medical unit includes both the first day and the last day (as 'lost' to the Army) and the average duration of each admission was 17·2 days. Taken over the whole group of healthy and unhealthy alike, the average days lost were 12·2 or 6·1 days per annum—a figure very similar to that reported in *The Young Wage-Earner* and not unlike the rate of incapacity for work among the insured population of Scotland of similar age during the 1930s, when records were available.

These figures represent in each year an admission rate of about 36 per cent. The totals in each year are deceptively equal, although the composition by diseases is quite unlike. In any consideration of admissions to medical treatment the geographical distribution of the areas in which the Service is being carried out are clearly important. Some broad indication of this has already been given; the periods of Service abroad are not accurately known, but generally speaking they would lie in the later part of the period of Service. Thus, there are the conflicting tendencies that in the first year the young men of 18 have the higher sickness-rate associated with initial Army Service, but this is at the lower level prevailing in the United Kingdom; while in the second year of Service the rate, which would otherwise tend to be lower, is increased by the new risks of Service overseas.

TABLE 4

Conditions chiefly responsible for admission to Army medical units in each of the two years of Service

Disease	First Year		Second Year	
	Cases	Days	Cases	Days
Tuberculosis, respiratory . . .	..	..	1	202
Venereal diseases	..	..	13	125
Dysentery	..	..	2	57
Rubella, &c.	3	32	..	..
Infective hepatitis	..	..	1	61
Malaria	..	..	2	29
Psychiatric conditions . . .	4	120	1	67
Eye conditions	5	50	..	..
Otitis externa and media . . .	2	18	1	11
Common cold	4	19	3	16
Tonsillitis and pharyngitis, acute .	9	56	3	40
Influenza	4	36	2	17
Pneumonia	1	8	2	69
Bronchitis	2	12	..	..
Teeth, diseases of	3	12	4	19
Hernia	2	111	4	128
Enteritis, diarrhoea, &c. . . .	2	9	2	36
Skin conditions (including tinea) .	20	338	17	391
Other diseases	22	533	25	252
Injuries	8	165	9	119
Total	91	1,519	92	1,639

There was no correlation between frequency of admission to medical units during Service and the amount of working time that had been lost through illness between the ages of 14 and 17 in civil life, nor between frequency of hospital admission during Service and extent of unemployment between the ages of 14 and 17.

7

Height and weight at entry to, and on leaving, the Army, in relation to height and weight on leaving school

It has been possible to compare, against a control group of National Servicemen drawn from the country as a whole, the average height and weight of the men in this study who did their National Service in the Army; the comparison is summarized in Table 5.

TABLE 5

Average height and weight at entry to, and on leaving, the Army: men in this study compared with a control group for whom all measurements were available from time of Ministry of Labour examination onwards

	Men in this study		Control group	
	Height	*Weight*	*Height*	*Weight*
Entry . .	66·2″	130·0 lb.	67·6″	135·8 lb.
Release .	66·9″	141·5 lb.	68·5″	148·0 lb.

These figures show that the Glasgow boys included in this study were on average shorter and lighter than other National Servicemen when they were called up, the weight difference being accounted for mainly by the difference in height. (S. Rosenbaum has noted that height is the important discriminator.[1]) The gain in weight during Service was substantial; on release the Glasgow group was in relatively the same position as the control group.

When the average height of the lads on leaving school was compared with the average height of the same lads (*a*) on entry, and (*b*) on leaving the Army, it was found that those who were taller on leaving school were also, on average, taller in the Army.

The same relationship between average height on leaving school and average height on release from Service was also found among the lads who served in the Royal Air Force.

In weight a similar correlation was observed: the boys who were heavier on leaving school were also, on average, heavier on release from the Army.

[1] S. Rosenbaum, 'Heights and Weights of the Army Intake, 1951', *J.R. Statist. Soc.*, 1954, A, **117**, iii. 331–47.

TABLE 6

Height on leaving school compared with height on entry to, and on leaving, the Army

Height on leaving school (inches)	No. of men	Average height on entry to Army (inches)	Average height on release from Army (inches)
Under 53	14	62·7	63·8
53–	17	63·8	65·1
54–	15	64·7	65·5
55–	17	64·6	65·4
56–	20	66·0	67·2
57–	23	66·1	67·0
58–	29	67·0	67·7
59–	25	67·3	68·1
60–	22	67·3	67·7
61–	13	69·1	70·3
62–	13	69·0	69·9
63 and over . . .	10	69·2	69·7
Average height 57·6 . . .	218	66·4	67·2

TABLE 7

Weight on leaving school compared with weight on entry to, and on leaving, the Army

Weight on leaving school (pounds)	No. of men	Average weight on entry into Army (pounds)	Average weight on release from Army (pounds)
Under 60	5	117	131
60–	8	105	113
65–	13	111	126
70–	21	119	136
75–	25	123	135
80–	37	129	141
85–	37	134	146
90–	27	138	149
95–	15	139	148
100–	12	140	150
105 and over . . .	18	154	164
Average weight 85·85 . . .	218	130·35	142·34

4

How the Men fared between the Ages of 20 and 22

I

Re-entry to civilian employment on return from Service

FULLY two-thirds of the men who had been away on Service resumed civil employment within a month of returning home; only 6 per cent. had not yet gone back to work 2 months after return to civil life. Nearly 62 per cent. of the 315 men who had completed 2 years' Service returned to their pre-Service job, but the proportion who went back to the kind of work they had been doing before they went away was appreciably higher among those who had served in the Royal Air Force (73 per cent.) than among those who had served in the Army (59 per cent.). One hundred and eighty-nine (60 per cent.) of the men who had been on Service returned to work with their pre-Service employer; only a handful of those who returned to the kind of job on which they had been engaged before going on Service changed their employer on return. Fully 28 per cent. of the men returned intending to complete an apprenticeship or period of training which they had interrupted to go on Service.

2

Difficulty in settling down in civil life

Just over one-fifth of the men (21·1 per cent.) reported that they had experienced difficulty in settling back into civil life on their return from Service. The difficulties which they encountered were mainly associated with employment—an aversion from returning to the job which they had left, because of either its nature or its lack of prospects, and difficulty in getting one they liked better. Sometimes the job itself would have pleased them well enough, but the wage that went with it did not appeal to them; sometimes, indeed, their family responsibilities had increased to a point that rendered change of job necessary. In a few cases the difficulties experienced were of a domestic nature: sometimes they turned on difficulty of adaptation to the altered values implicit in a return to civil life. There was virtually no difference, in the proportion of men reporting difficulty in settling in, between those who had served in the Royal Air Force and those who had served in the Army. As was to be expected, the proportion of men who reported difficulty in settling was much lower among those who returned to their old jobs than among those who did not—14·5 per cent. as against 31·7 per cent.

3

The type of work in which the men were employed

At the beginning of the 2-year period of study, when the men were 20 years of age, 92 (29·3 per cent.) of the 314 returned Servicemen for whom information was available were still serving an apprenticeship or undergoing a period of training. In addition 10 (3·2 per cent.) had completed training and were employed as journeymen in skilled manual work. It will be remembered that, while they were on Service, 14 of the men had received training which was accepted as contributing to their apprenticeship.

At the age of 20, 60 of the men (19·1 per cent.) were employed in semi-skilled work; 93 (29·6 per cent.) were unskilled labourers; 44 (14·0 per cent.) were engaged in non-manual work; and 15 (4·8 per cent.) were unemployed. There was no difference in the proportion of men who were in skilled work at the age of 20 between those who had served in the Royal Air Force and those who had served in the Army; but the proportion who were unskilled labourers was higher among those who had done their Service in the Army (32 per cent. as against 19 per cent.) and, on the other hand, the proportion in non-manual work was higher among those who had served in the Royal Air Force (22 per cent. as against 11·5 per cent.).

The nature of the work to which the men came back on their return from Service made comparatively little difference to the ease with which they settled back into civil life. Thus, 18 per cent. of those who had returned to complete apprenticeships or periods of training reported difficulty in settling in; 24 per cent. of those who came back to semi-skilled work; 23 per cent. of those who were in unskilled jobs; and 20 per cent. of those who had been in non-manual work before going on Service.

4

The employment position 2 years after return from Service

At the end of the 2-year period of study, when the men were 22 years of age, 26 (8·6 per cent.) of the 303 men returned from Service, for whom information on this point was available, were still serving an apprenticeship or period of training, and 47 (15·5 per cent.), having completed an apprenticeship, were employed as journeymen in skilled manual work; 93 (30·7 per cent.) were in semi-skilled work; 86 (28·4 per cent.) were unskilled manual labourers; 47 (15·5 per cent.) were in non-manual work; and 4 (1·3 per cent.) were unemployed. Then, as 2 years previously, there was a relative excess of men employed as unskilled labourers among those who had done their Service in the Army—32 per cent. as against 16 per cent. of the men who had done their Service in the Royal Air Force. On the other hand, there was a relative excess of non-manual workers among those who had done their Service in the Royal Air Force (25 per cent. as against 12·5 per cent.).

5

Nature of employment of men rejected as unfit for National Service

Among the 222 men who had been rejected as medically unfit for National Service and had remained in civil life, the status of employment at the age of 20 was that 42 (18·9 per cent.) were still serving apprenticeships and 10 (4·5 per cent.), having completed their apprenticeships, were engaged as journeymen in skilled manual work; 48 (21·6 per cent.) were in semi-skilled work; 84 (37·8 per cent.) were unskilled labourers; 23 (10·4 per cent.) were in non-manual work; and 15 (6·8 per cent.) were unemployed.

At the end of the 2-year period of study, when the men were 22 years of age, of the 218 for whom information was available 4 (1·8 per cent.) were still in process of completing apprenticeship; 35 (16·1 per cent.) had completed their training and were employed as journeymen in skilled manual work; 47 (21·6 per cent.) were employed in semi-skilled work; 92 (42·2 per cent.) were unskilled manual labourers; 26 (11·9 per cent.) were in non-manual work; and 14 (6·4 per cent.) were unemployed.

6

The occupation of men who had been on Service compared with that of men rejected as unfit for National Service

Table 8 summarizes the position: it shows that, both at the beginning and at the end of the 2-year period of study, the proportion of men in skilled manual work, or in process of acquiring skill, was higher among the men who had been on Service than among those who had been rejected on medical grounds. It shows, too, that in both groups there was a considerable decline in the proportion of men in skilled manual work at the end of the 2 years as compared with the beginning —taking together those serving apprenticeships or periods of training and those who, having completed such periods, were employed in skilled manual work—and that the extent of the decline was only slightly greater among those who had been on Service. The proportion of men who were unskilled manual labourers was consistently higher among those who had been rejected on medical grounds and the proportion in non-manual work consistently lower. The proportion of unemployed men was higher among those who had been rejected on medical grounds than among those who had been on Service. Before the groups can be directly compared, the true significance of these findings has to be considered in the light of the earlier social, environmental, and occupational background of the men. This will be done in Chapter 5.

Fourteen of the lads who had been serving apprenticeships or undergoing periods of training at the age of 20 were engaged in non-manual work at the age of 22: 5 of them had done their National Service in the Army and 5 in the Royal Air Force; 4 were among the medical rejects. Of those who had served in the Army, 2 were working at the age of 22 in the employment for which they had been in course of training at the age of 20, 3 in some other type of non-manual work; of those who had served in the Royal Air Force, 4 were working at the age of 20 as they had been trained and one in some other kind of non-manual work; those who had been medically rejected were all working as trained. The overall position was that, at age 20, 32·5 per cent. of the men who had been on Service were employed in skilled manual work or were in process of training, whereas at age 22 only 24·1 per cent. were so employed—74·2 per cent. of the earlier figure. Of the men who, having been rejected as unfit for Service, remained in civil life, 23·4 per cent.

TABLE 8

Nature of employment at beginning of study and at end (percentage distribution): ex-National Servicemen and medical rejects compared

	At age 20		At age 22	
Nature of employment	*Ex-National Servicemen (314)*	*Medical rejects (222)*	*Ex-National Servicemen (303)*	*Medical rejects (218)*
Undergoing apprenticeship or period of training	29·3	18·9	8·6	1·8
Skilled manual	3·2	4·5	15·5	16·1
Semi-skilled manual	19·1	21·6	30·7	21·6
Unskilled manual	29·6	37·8	28·4	42·2
Non-manual	14·0	10·4	15·5	11·9
Unemployed	4·8	6·8	1·3	6·4
	100·0	100·0	100·0	100·0

were at age 20 employed in skilled manual work or were in process of training, whereas at age 22 the corresponding proportion was 17·9 per cent., a reduction to some 76·5 per cent. of the earlier figure; so that the proportion who fell out of skilled work between the ages of 20 and 22 was rather higher among those who had been away on Service than among those who had remained in civil life.

7

Earnings

It was possible to ascertain with reasonable accuracy the weekly wages of about 90 per cent. of the men at the age of 20 and of about 80 per cent. at the age of 22. There was no significant difference in the amount of the gross weekly wage received by men who had been on Service as compared with those who had not: at the age of 22 the proportion earning more than 160s. a week was slightly higher among those rejected on medical grounds, but the proportion earning less than 120*s*. a week was also rather higher among them. The general level of wages was, of course, appreciably higher at the age of 22 than at the age of 20.

There was little difference in gross weekly earnings at the age of 22 between men who had served in the Royal Air Force and those who had done their Service in the Army, except that the proportion of men who were earning less than 120*s*. a week

TABLE 9

Gross weekly earnings at age 20 and at age 22 (percentage distribution):
ex-National Servicemen and medical rejects compared

	At age 20		At age 22	
Gross weekly earnings	*Ex-National Servicemen* (*297*)	*Medical rejects* (*193*)	*Ex-National Servicemen* (*269*)	*Medical rejects* (*176*)
Under 80*s*.	5·5	4·1	..	..
80*s*.	66·5	60·2	10·8	14·2
120*s*.	24·8	32·6	74·4	68·8
160*s*.	2·2	3·1	12·6	13·6
200*s*. and over . . .	1·0	..	2·2	3·4
	100·0	100·0	100·0	100·0

was greater among those who had been in the Army, 12 per cent. as against 6 per cent.

8

Unemployment

Overall, the amount of working time lost through unemployment between the ages of 20 and 22 was very similar among the men who had been on Service and among those who, having been rejected on medical grounds as unfit for Service, remained in civil life. In both the 'Service' and 'rejected' groups some 62 per cent. of the men lost no working time through unemployment in the course of 2 years; 11 or 12 per cent. lost less than 4 weeks during that period; a further 11 per cent. lost 4 to 8 weeks; 4 per cent. lost from 9 to 12 weeks; and about 11 per cent. were unemployed for more than 3 months in the course of the 24. But men who had served in the Royal Air Force suffered much less unemployment during the 2 years than men who had served in the Army; of the former group 81 per cent. experienced no unemployment, of the latter 58 per cent., and the ex-soldiers suffered nearly twice as much 'long-term' unemployment, extending to 2 months or more in the course of the 2 years.

Men who had returned to their pre-Service job on leaving the Forces experienced less unemployment than men who took up other work. Among those who served in the Royal Air Force, for example, 88 per cent. of those who returned to their pre-Service job wholly escaped unemployment between the ages of 20 and 22, as compared with only 56 per cent. of those who went to other work. Similarly, among those who served in the Army, 68 per cent. of those who returned to pre-Service jobs wholly escaped unemployment between the ages of 20 and 22, as compared with only 43 per cent. of those who took up other jobs on return.

As was to be expected, unemployment and difficulty in settling back into civil life went hand-in-hand; thus, among men who did their Service in the Royal Air Force only 15 per cent. of those who wholly escaped unemployment during the 2 years of this study had complained of difficulty in settling back into civil life, and 71 per cent. of those who experienced unemployment had done so. Among those who had done their Service in the Army, the experience was similar; 14 per cent. of those without unemployment in the course of the 2 years had complained of difficulty in settling in, as against 33 per cent. who suffered some unemployment.

The incidence and severity of unemployment varied with the nature of the work in which the men were engaged on return to civil life. Unemployment occurred most frequently among unskilled manual labourers. The men who had done their National Service in the Royal Air Force were found to have escaped unemployment more frequently than men who had been rejected on medical grounds, the gap being widest among skilled manual workers, narrowest among unskilled labourers. Men who had served in the Army, on the other hand, experienced unemployment after expiry of their 'reinstatement rights' more frequently than men who had done their Service in the Royal Air Force, and more frequently, over the same period, than men who had been rejected as unfit for National Service and had therefore remained at home.

Similarly, unemployment, when it did occur, tended to be of longer duration among unskilled manual labourers; and unskilled manual labourers who had been on Service were more prone to prolonged unemployment than unskilled manual workers who had been rejected as unfit for National Service. Thus, 25 per cent. of the men who had been on Service and who were working as unskilled manual labourers on return to civil life

TABLE 10

The proportion of men who experienced no unemployment between the ages of 20½ and 22 in relation to the nature of employment in which they were engaged at age 20: showing separately the experience of men who had done National Service in the Army and in the Royal Air Force and men who had been rejected as medically unfit for Service

	Percentage who escaped unemployment		
Nature of work at age 20	Served in Army (244)	Served in Royal Air Force (68)	Rejected as unfit for Service (222)
Skilled or undergoing apprenticeship	65	87	67
Semi-skilled manual . . .	65	82	74
Unskilled manual . . .	43	62	61
Non-manual	61	85	76

experienced more than 2 months of unemployment in the course of the 18 months immediately following the expiry of their period of 'reinstatement rights', whereas in the 18 months between the ages of 20½ and 22 only 18 per cent. of those in unskilled manual labour who had been rejected as unfit for National Service had suffered unemployment of comparable duration.

9

Frequency of change of job

Among both groups of men—those who had been away on National Service and those who had not—there was a good deal of changing of jobs in the course of the study. During the first 6 months after their return to civil life, 84·8 per cent. of the men who had been on Service stayed in one job without change, doubtless sometimes because of the operation of 'reinstatement rights'. During a comparable period of 6 months only 68·8 per cent. of the men who had been rejected for National Service did not change their job. But 6 months later the gap had narrowed considerably. By the end of the first year after their return 35 per cent. of the men who had been away on National Service had changed their job at least once. Of those who had been rejected as unfit for Service 43 per cent. changed their job at least once in the course of the year when they were between 20 and 21 years of age.

A year later, at the end of the second year after their return, only 46 per cent. of those who had been away on Service had had no change of job, almost exactly the same proportion as that observed during a comparable period of 2 years among the men who had been rejected as unfit for National Service.

Over the period of 2 years 4 per cent. of the men who had been on Service changed their jobs four or more times; the corresponding figure for the men rejected as unfit was 13·9 per cent.

Change of job during the 2 years occurred much less frequently where the Serviceman returned to his pre-Service job: of Royal Air Force men who so returned 38 per cent. changed their jobs at least once during the 2 years, whereas of those who took up new jobs on return to civil life 76 per cent. changed their jobs. Among men who had done their Service in the Army 50 per cent. of those who returned to their old work remained in it throughout the period of study as compared with 34 per cent. of those who took up new work.

As was to be expected, the men who complained of difficulty in settling down on return to civil life were those who changed their jobs most frequently during the 2 years after return: 77 per cent. of the airmen who experienced difficulty in settling changed jobs at least once in the course of the 2 years, but only 41 per cent. of those who reported no difficulty in settling. Similarly, 72 per cent. of those men who had served in the Army and complained of difficulty in settling in civil life changed jobs at least once, but only 49 per cent. of those who settled in without difficulty.

Frequency of change of job between the ages of 20 and 22 was related to the nature of the work on which the man was engaged at the age of 20: men in skilled work made fewer changes than unskilled men. Thus, among the men who had done their Service in the Royal Air Force 65 per cent. of those in skilled work at the beginning of this study had no change of job during the 2 years, as compared with only 30 per cent. of those in unskilled work. Among the men who had done their Service in the Army 57 per cent. of those in skilled work at the beginning of this study had no change of job during the 2 years, as compared with only 35 per cent. of those in unskilled work.

Among men who had been rejected as medically unfit for Service this difference was not so wide; 55 per cent. of those in skilled work at the beginning of the period had not changed jobs during the 2 years as against 48 per cent. of those in unskilled work.

10

Time lost through illness

Over the 2 years covered by the study there were wide differences between the two groups—those who had been on Service and those who had been rejected as unfit—in the amount of working time lost through illness. Those who had been rejected as unfit for Service on medical grounds experienced much more illness during that period than those who had been on Service.

TABLE 11

Extent of incapacity for work on account of illness in the course of 2 years (percentage distribution): ex-National Servicemen and medical rejects compared

Time lost through illness in the course of 2 years	Ex-National Servicemen (298)	Medical rejects (220)
None	75·3	53·1
Less than 4 weeks . .	14·2	22·3
4–8 weeks . . .	7·4	10·9
9–12 weeks . .	2·4	3·2
13 weeks or more . .	0·7	10·5
	100·0	100·0

The excess of prolonged incapacity in the course of the 2 years among those who had been rejected for National Service is striking: of those who had been off work on account of illness for 3 months or more during that time eight were cases of pulmonary tuberculosis and two of non-pulmonary tuberculosis, three of chest disease not known to be tuberculous, two of mastoid suppuration, and one each of disseminated sclerosis, duodenal ulcer, rheumatic heart disease, dermatitis, and enlarged thymus; for the three remaining cases the cause of incapacity was not stated, but two of the lads were described as of 'poor physique'.

There was little variation with the nature of employment in the proportion of men who entirely escaped sickness-absence in the course of the 2 years (except that those unemployed at the age of 20 had more than their share of sickness-absence during the 2 following years): prolonged sickness-absence was most common among those who had been unskilled manual labourers at the age of 20 and among those who had been unemployed. These findings applied alike to returned Servicemen and to the men rejected as unfit for National Service on medical grounds.

II

Working time lost through illness compared with that lost through unemployment

It has already been seen that during the 2 years after return to civil life those men who had done their Service in the Army suffered much more unemployment than those who had done Service in the Royal Air Force, and that the experience of the men who had remained in civil life lay somewhere between. On the other hand, the proportion of men who wholly escaped incapacity for work during the 2 years of this study was appreciably higher among those who had been called up for Service than among those who had been rejected on medical grounds as unfit for National Service (Table 11): the incidence of sickness-absence during the 2 years differed little between the men who had served in the Army and those who had served in the Royal Air Force.

It is interesting, therefore, to consider the amount of unemployment experienced during the 2 years by the three series of men—those who served in the Army, those who served in the Royal Air Force, and those rejected as unfit for Service—in the light of the amount of incapacity for work on account of illness experienced by each group during the same period. When that is done, the better overall record of the ex-airmen in relation to unemployment as compared with the men rejected as unfit for National Service is seen to be confined entirely to those men who remained free of incapacitating sickness during the period: among the ex-airmen who had lost working time through illness the proportion who escaped unemployment was actually lower than the corresponding proportion among those rejected as unfit for National Service. The experience of ex-soldiers was similar; less than half of those who had lost some working time through sickness in the course of the 2 years had escaped unemployment over the same period.

TABLE 12

Percentage of men who escaped unemployment throughout this study: those who did not lose working time through illness during the period compared with those who did; ex-Servicemen and medical rejects shown separately

	Percentage who escaped unemployment	
	Of those who lost working time through illness during the period	*Of those not incapacitated by illness during the period*
Served in Royal Air Force .	90	56
Served in Army . . .	64	41
All National Servicemen . .	69	45
Rejected as unfit for National Service	61	64

Where there had been no time lost through illness in the course of the 2 years, the proportion of men who escaped unemployment was appreciably better among those who had been rejected as unfit for Service than among those who had been away on Service.

12

Civil state

When they were visited in their homes at the age of 20, 2·9 per cent. of the men recently returned from National Service were already married, and among the men who had been rejected as unfit for National Service the proportion already married was 7·2 per cent. At the age of 22 the balance had not been wholly restored; then, 17·7 per cent. of the ex-National Servicemen and 21·4 per cent. of those rejected as unfit for Service were married.

In agreement with these findings, 96·5 per cent. of those who had returned from Service were, at the time of the first visit, living in their parents' homes, 1·9 per cent. were in lodgings, and 1·3 per cent. in homes of their own; one was at sea. At the age of 22, 82·3 per cent. of the men who had completed National Service were still living in their parents' home, 6·5 per cent. were in lodgings, and 10·5 per cent. were in homes of their own: two were living 'otherwise'. Among those who had been rejected as unfit for National Service, 92·3 per cent. were living with their parents at the time of the first visit, 4·1 per cent. were in lodgings, and 1·8 per cent. in homes of their own. At the age of 22, 77·1 per cent. were still living with their parents, 9·6 per cent. were in lodgings, and 11·0 per cent. were in homes of their own: two or three were living in 'other' kinds of accommodation.

13

Type of housing district in which the men lived

The type of housing district in which the men lived changed comparatively little during the 2 years this study was in progress. In general, a lower proportion of the men who had been rejected as unfit for National Service on medical grounds lived in 'good' or 'fair' working-class districts of the older type; a relatively high proportion of this group lived in 'poor' housing districts of older types, or in areas that were frankly slums. There was an interesting difference in housing-area distribution between men who had done their Service in the Royal Air Force and those who had served in the Army. Among those who had served in the Royal Air Force, a much larger proportion lived in 'good' or 'fair' housing districts of the older type, with relatively few in 'poor' or 'slum' old houses or in 'new' local-authority housing schemes. Table 13 summarizes the position.

Among the men who were living in 'good' or 'fair' houses of the older type, or in 'new' local-authority houses, the proportion who were engaged in skilled manual work was substantially higher than among those living in 'poor' or 'slum' houses of the older type; and, in general, the proportion in unskilled labouring work was substantially lower.

As has been shown (Table 8), the proportion of men employed in skilled manual work was considerably higher among the ex-Servicemen than among the men rejected as unfit for National Service. Yet the proportion of skilled manual workers among those of the rejected men who were living in 'good' or

TABLE 13

Type of housing district at age 20, showing separately the kind of area of residence of men who had done National Service in the Royal Air Force and in the Army and of men rejected as unfit for National Service

Type of housing district	Served in Royal Air Force (68)	Served in Army (222)	Rejected as unfit for National Service (208)
	(%)	(%)	(%)
Working class, 'good' or 'fair' .	57·3	35·1	32·7
Working class, 'poor' or 'slum' .	10·6	20·3	24·0
'New' local-authority housing scheme	31·8	43·2	40·9
Other	0·3	1·4	2·4
	100·0	100·0	100·0

'fair' working-class districts of the older type was just as high as that among the ex-Servicemen who lived in similar types of housing districts. On the other hand, the proportion working as unskilled labourers was higher among the rejected men who lived in 'good' or 'fair' working-class districts of the older type than among the ex-Servicemen who lived in similar types of district.

There was no significant difference with type of housing district in the proportion of men who wholly escaped unemployment during the 2 years while the study was in progress, but the weight of prolonged unemployment (more than 2 months in the course of the 2 years) was heaviest among those who lived in 'poor' or 'slum' houses of older type; this was true alike of men who had been away on National Service and of those who had been rejected as unfit.

There was no difference with type of housing district in the frequency with which men changed their jobs during the study.

Nor was there any substantial variation with type of housing district in the proportion of men who had no sickness-absence in the course of the 2 years. In each type of district about 50 per cent. of the men who had been rejected as unfit for Service had no sickness-absence during the 2 years; among the men who had returned from Service fully 70 per cent. in each type of housing district had no sickness-absence. Similarly, there was little correlation between protracted sickness-absence—exceeding 2 months in the course of 2 years—and the type of housing district.

14
Severity of overcrowding in the home

Severe overcrowding in the home was found to be rather less prevalent at the end of the study (when the men were 22 years of age) than it had been at the beginning (when they were 20), chiefly because some who had married in the course of the 2 years had come from severely overcrowded homes. Even if they started married life in a single sub-let room, as often happened, the ratio of persons per room was less than it had been in their family home. At the end of this study, 14 per cent. of those who had been rejected as unfit for National Service were living under conditions of crowding of three persons or more per room: among the men who had been on Service, the corresponding figure was 10·3 per cent.; but it was 12·3 per cent. for the group of the ex-soldiers and 4·5 per cent. for the group of the ex-airmen.

Where overcrowding in the home was severe, the proportion of men employed in skilled manual work tended to be low. This held true for men rejected as unfit for National Service as well as for men who had completed their Service, irrespective of the Service in which they had been. Thus, among men rejected on medical grounds, of those living under conditions of less than two persons per room, 28 per cent. were employed in skilled manual work; but among those living under conditions of more severe crowding only 18 per cent. were in skilled manual work. Among the ex-airmen who lived under conditions of less than two persons per room 43 per cent. were in skilled manual work; but among those crowded to the extent of two persons per room or worse only 24 per cent. were in skilled manual work. Among ex-soldiers who lived under conditions of less than two persons per room 37 per cent. were in skilled manual work; among those crowded to the extent of two or more persons per room only 26 per cent. were skilled manual workers.

15

Membership of an organized social group

At the beginning of this study, on their return from Service, 11·8 per cent. of the men who had been called up were members of an organized social group, some of a football or cycling club, some of a social organization attached to a church, some were associated with such activities as the Boys' Brigade, Boy Scouts, or boys' clubs. As a general rule, these associations were a re-establishment of connexions that had already existed before the men went on Service rather than entirely new interests developed after return. The proportion of men who were members of an organized social group was much higher among those who had done their Service in the Royal Air Force (26 per cent.) than among those who had served in the Army (7 per cent.). Among the men who had been rejected as unfit for Service, and who therefore had an opportunity of preserving unbroken any existing ties with social organizations, 19·5 per cent. were members of a group of this kind.

Among men rejected as unfit for National Service the occupational group that yielded the highest proportion attached to an organized social group was that of skilled manual workers, of whom nearly 40 per cent. belonged to a club when they were 20 years of age. Among men who had returned from Service, on the other hand, the skilled manual workers did not contribute largely to club membership, only about 8 per cent. being attached to a group.

16

The use of leisure

In the course of this study the men were asked about their spare-time interests and the way in which they used their leisure time. Seven of the 315 lads who had been on Service and two of the 222 who had been rejected as unfit for Service said they had no leisure interests.

Many of the lads had several interests. Football (as either player or spectator), cinema, and dancing were easily at the top of the list; then followed a wide range of activities:

Leisure interests	Service (315)	Rejected (222)	*Leisure interests*	Service (315)	Rejected (222)
Football	166	103	Other crafts . .	3	9
'Pictures'	145	114	Odd jobs at home .	7	9
Dancing	131	87	Minding baby .	2	2
Reading	56	34	Athletics . .	7	4
Courting	44	35	Religion . .	8	3
Cycling	32	40	Clubs . . .	11	4
Motor cycling . . .	9	8	Theatre . .	5	5
Swimming	23	10	Photography . .	2	5
'Territorials'	30	..	Camping, youth		
Music	11	15	hostelling .	4	2
Collecting gramophone records .	4	4	Speedway . .	3	3
Radio and television . . .	14	13	Fishing . .	2	3
Billiards and snooker . .	13	10	Breeding animals .	2	1
Skating	15	8	Drawing . .	2	1
Golf	14	8	Ice hockey . .	2	1
Evening classes . . .	10	10	Politics . .	1	2
Walking, hiking . . .	7	10	Civil defence . .	..	2
Tennis, table tennis, badminton .	12	4	Shooting . .	..	2
Woodwork	5	7	Basketball . .	2	..

The list hardly does justice to the variety of leisure interests. For example, among lads who had been on Service, the following interests were each mentioned once:

Bowls	Pigeons
Darts	'Motors'
Chess	Rowing
Gardening	Farm work

and among the interests mentioned by those who had been rejected as unfit for Service were some that were even more colourful:

Acting	Petty thieving
Looking for better job	Pubs
Card playing	Driving tractor

There was little difference in the chief interests of the two groups; but cycling, radio, hiking, woodwork, and other crafts seemed to appeal particularly to the lads who had been rejected as unfit for Service, while skating, tennis, badminton, golf, and athletics made relatively more appeal to the lads who had returned from Service.

Only ten men in each of the two groups—Service and non-Service—attended evening classes between the ages of 20 and 22.

5

The Influence of Earlier
Background on the Success of Men
between the Ages of 20 and 22

I

The importance of earlier influences

THE Carnegie surveyors, in their study of youth and early
manhood during the industrial depression of the 1930s, found
that the malaise of 20-year-olds in those days very often had its
roots farther back—that very often the damage was done in the
immediately post-school years. We, in turn, found (as reported
in *The Young Wage-Earner*) that the success of lads between the
ages of 14 and 17 was influenced, and often governed, by the
circumstances of earlier home life and schooldays; and it is
natural that in this study of young manhood in a happier
economic setting we should look again at the influence of
earlier events on later developments. It has, indeed, long been
taken as axiomatic that the early years of life are the most
fruitful in shaping a career. Even in relation to some of the
events of National Service itself, earlier social and environmental factors have been shown to play a part in shaping a lad's
attitude to Service, and his prospects of promotion in it.

National Service cannot fail to be a major event in the life of
any young man called upon to undertake it. It can be, and
sometimes is, a great force, for good or for evil. Yet there is a
good deal of evidence that the reaction of young men to
National Service is very often heavily coloured by much the
same basic social and environmental factors as were found to
play a large part in determining the success or failure of young
men between the ages of 14 and 17, or the success or failure in
their early twenties of many of the lads who were rejected as
unfit for National Service and therefore remained in civil life.
Some of the elements in National Service seem to influence
subsequent events surprisingly little; in this sense, Service over-

seas, for instance, appeared to influence scarcely at all the ease or difficulty of settling back into civil life. Similarly, the nature of the duties undertaken by the Serviceman while he was away seemed to influence very little the ease with which he re-established himself on his return; the men who were on 'trade' duties while on Service were among those who said they experienced most difficulty on return.

2

The stabilizing influence of return to pre-Service job

One major stabilizing factor in resettlement was the ability or inclination of the returned Serviceman to go back to his immediate pre-Service job. Those who had been serving an apprenticeship when they went away on Service were those who most often returned to their old job; among those who had served in the Royal Air Force, 18 out of 21 who had been serving apprenticeships returned to them, and, among those who had served in the Army, 62 out of 82. Among those who had been in non-manual work—chiefly clerical or distributive—before going on Service, the proportion returning to old jobs was lower: 22 out of 30 among those who had served in the Royal Air Force and 27 out of 47 among those who had served in the Army. There was no difference in frequency of return to the old job between those who had been members of an organized social group before going on Service and those who had not been members of such a group: and membership of a group before going on Service seemed to play no significant part in determining the ease with which a man settled back into civil life at the end of his Service.

The men who least frequently complained of difficulty in settling into civil life were those who had 'skilled' jobs (or apprenticeships) to which they returned: 19 of 105 'skilled' men (18 per cent.) complained of difficulty in settling, compared with 20 out of 86 unskilled (23 per cent.) and 17 out of 82 non-manual workers (21 per cent.).

3

Frequency of change of job

Frequency of change of job between the ages of 20 and 22 did not vary greatly with the level of scholastic ability on leaving

E

school, though it was interesting—both among men called up and among those rejected as unfit—that a relatively high proportion of men in group 'C' (that is, intermediate in point of scholastic ability) had not changed their jobs at all during these years, and that in groups 'A' and 'B' (the best) and groups 'D' and 'E' (the worst) fewer had stayed in one job throughout the two years.

Both among men called up for National Service and among men registered as unfit for Service those who had most frequently changed their jobs between the ages of 14 and 17 also changed jobs most frequently between the ages of 20 and 22. In general, the proportion of men who stayed in the same job over the entire period of 2 years between the ages of 20 and 22 was much the same among those called up for Service and among those rejected as unfit (about half of the total in each group); but among those rejected there was a group (over 13 per cent.) who had four or more changes in the course of the 2 years, whereas among the ex-Servicemen there was a much smaller proportion (less than 4 per cent.) with a similarly high frequency of change. This small group of men with many changes of job between the ages of 20 and 22 tended to contain more than its fair share of those who had changed their jobs very frequently between the ages of 14 and 17.

4

Occupational status at the age of 22 in the light of earlier circumstances

One way of trying to estimate the impact of earlier events on the subsequent performance of these young men is to consider their occupational status at the age of 22, two years after return from Service—by which time they should have had a reasonable opportunity of settling down—in the light of earlier circumstances.

Consider first the relationship between the occupational status of these young men of 22 and the category in which they had been placed in point of physical assessment when they left school. Among the men returned from National Service the proportion employed in skilled manual work at the age of 22 was higher in the group of those classified as of 'good' physique when they left school than in the other groups; but this did not hold among lads who had been rejected as unfit for National Service.

Neither among men called up for National Service nor among those rejected as unfit was there much correlation between physical assessment on leaving school and employment on unskilled manual work at the age of 22; the hard physical effort involved in many labouring jobs introduced an element of selection, but many lads of poorish physical condition had drifted into heavy and precarious unskilled work with a prospect of subsequent health breakdown and unemployment.

There was a tendency for the ranks of those who were unemployed at the age of 22 to be overloaded with lads who had been classified as of 'fair' or 'poor' general physique on leaving school.

The position among men who were engaged in non-manual work at the age of 22 was more obscure, probably because the label 'non-manual' covers a wide range of occupations, some skilled and of good prospects, attracting good recruits, and others inferior and without prospects, attracting only lads of poor quality.

TABLE 14

Proportion (as a percentage) of men engaged in various types of work at age 22, classified according to the physical category in which they had been placed on leaving school: men who had done National Service shown separately from men rejected as unfit for National Service

Physical assessment on leaving school	Service	Nature of work at age 22				
		Skilled manual	Semi-skilled manual	Un-skilled manual	Non-manual	Un-employed
'A' (good) . .	Served in Army (83) . .	28	35	29	7	1
	,, Royal Air Force (21) .	29	19	19	33	0
	Rejected as unfit (58) . .	16	20	45	16	3
'B', 'C' (fair or poor) .	Served in Army (161) . .	21	34	31	14	0
	,, Royal Air Force (47) .	24	30	19	21	6
	Rejected as unfit (159) . .	17	23	41	11	8

5

Nature of employment at the age of 22 in relation to height on leaving school

When the nature of employment in which they were engaged at the age of 22 was set against the height of the lads concerned when they left school at the age of 14, the picture was very similar; among those who had been badly undersized (i.e. under 57 inches in height) at the age of 14, the proportion employed at the age of 22 in skilled manual and non-manual work was, in general, lower than among boys over that height. On the other hand, the proportion working as unskilled labourers tended to be greater among the undersized boys.

TABLE 15

Proportion (as a percentage) of men engaged in various types of work at age 22, classified according to their height on leaving school: men who had done National Service shown separately from men rejected as unfit for National Service

Height on leaving school*	Nature of work at age 22									
	Skilled manual		Semi-skilled		Unskilled manual		Non-manual		Unemployed	
	Served	Rejected	Served	Rejected	Served	Rejected	Served	Rejected	Served	Rejected
Under 57" (144) (86)	17	16	34	20	35	45	12	7	2	12
57"–58" (87) (40)	22	21	37	26	27	45	10	5	4	3
59"+ (113) (85)	31	16	27	23	19	36	19	20	4	5

* The figures in brackets in this column indicate the numbers of men in each height grouping who served and who were rejected as unfit for National Service.

6

Nature of employment at the age of 22 in relation to level of scholastic ability

As noted in Chapter 2, there was a much higher proportion of lads of poor scholastic ability among those rejected as unfit for National Service than among those called up for Service. Of those rejected, 55 per cent. had been placed on leaving school in categories 'D' or 'E' (the lowest) in point of scholastic ability, whereas the corresponding proportion among those who served for the ordinary period of 2 years was 43 per cent. to 45 per cent. among those who served in the Army and 32 per cent. among those who served in the Royal Air Force. There was a relationship between the level of scholastic ability of the lads when they left school and the kind of work in which they were engaged at the age of 22, as shown in Table 16.

In general, the proportion of men who were engaged in skilled manual work at the age of 22 fell with decline in the level of scholastic ability, as did the proportion of men in semi-skilled manual work and, to a lesser extent, the proportion of men in non-manual work. On the other hand, the proportion of men in unskilled labouring work increased as the level of scholastic ability fell. This was true both for men who had been on Service and for those who, having been rejected as unfit for Service, remained in civil life; but among those who had been rejected

TABLE 16

Proportion (as a percentage) of men engaged in various types of work at age 22, classified according to their level of scholastic ability on leaving school: men who had done National Service shown separately from those rejected as unfit for National Service

Scholastic assessment on leaving school*	Nature of work at age 22									
	Skilled manual		Semi-skilled		Unskilled manual		Non-manual		Unemployed	
	Served	Rejected	Served	Rejected	Served	Rejected	Served	Rejected	Served	Rejected
'A', 'B' (good) (36) (13) . .	30	38·5	26	38·5	26	8	18	15	..	..	=100
'C' (average) (143) (86) .	24	22]	30	26	24	36	19	11	3	5	=100
'D', 'E' (poor) (136) (121) . . .	22	14	34	16	34	50	10	12	..	8	=100

* The figures in brackets in this column indicate the number of men in each scholastic grouping who served and who were rejected as unfit for National Service.

as unfit for Service the deterioration in the proportion of men in skilled manual work as scholastic ability declined was more spectacular than among those who had been on Service.

Among the comparatively small group of men placed in categories 'A' and 'B' (the best) in scholastic ability, the proportion in skilled and semi-skilled manual work at the age of 22 was higher and the proportion in unskilled manual work lower among those rejected as unfit for National Service than among those called up. Among those in categories 'D' and 'E' (the worst) in scholastic ability, these positions were reversed.

7

Changes in job status between the ages of 17 and 22: men who had been on Service compared with men rejected as unfit for National Service

Next consider job status at 17 in relation to job status at 22, comparing the experience of men who had been away on

TABLE 17

Men engaged in various types of work at age 22 compared with the corresponding occupational distribution at age 17: men who had done National Service shown separately from men rejected as unfit for Service

| Kind of work at age 17 | Men returned from National Service | | | | | | Men rejected as unfit for National Service | | | | | |
| | Kind of work at age 22 | | | | | | Kind of work at age 22 | | | | | |
	Skilled manual	Semi-skilled	Unskilled manual	Non-manual	Unemployed	Total	Skilled manual	Semi-skilled	Unskilled manual	Non-manual	Unemployed	Total
Skilled manual (apprentices)	60	16	18	9	1	104	33	4	8	8	4	58
Semi-skilled	5	14	12	5	..	36	..	7	10	3	..	20
Unskilled manual	4	32	37	6	1	80	2	24	43	3	7	79
Non-manual	5	29	19	26	1	80	4	13	26	12	3	58
Unemployed	..	..	..	..	1	1	..	..	1	..	..	1
	74	91	86	46	4	301	39	48	89	26	14	216

Service with that of men rejected as unfit. Information is available for 301 of the men who were away on Service and for 216 of the rejected men, and the change in occupational distribution over the years is shown in Table 17.

Looking first at those who had been rejected as unfit for National Service, we find that the proportion employed in skilled work at the age of 22 was considerably lower than the proportion apprenticed at the age of 17; on the face of it, this is obviously a serious matter, which will call for further study. Eight of the boys who had been apprentices at the age of 17 were returned as being in non-manual work at the age of 22; four of the eight were then working in trades in which they had been trained (as grocers, &c.), but the other four were not in the kinds of job for which they had been trained. On the other hand, to offset some of this loss, two of the lads who were in unskilled work and four who were in non-manual work at the age of 17 were in process of training for skilled work at the age of 22: even so, the loss of skill over the 5 years is very considerable, something of the order of 26 per cent.

The number of men employed in non-manual work was much greater at the age of 17 than at the age of 22; the big drop in the number of lads in non-manual work between these ages probably represents a drifting away or dismissal of lads from stop-gap or dead-end jobs. On the other hand, at the age of 22 the number of men in semi-skilled work had gone up considerably and the number in unskilled manual work had increased slightly. There was, unhappily, a larger proportion of unemployed.

Among the men who had been away for 2 years on National Service the position was very similar. At the age of 17, 105 of the men in this group were serving apprenticeships or undergoing periods of training, but only 73 were in skilled manual work at the age of 22, though 3 of the others were working in non-manual work in which they had undergone a period of training. The number of men engaged in semi-skilled manual work at the age of 22 was more than double that in this type of work at the age of 17: the number of unskilled manual labourers was slightly higher at the age of 22 than at the age of 17; but the number of men in non-manual work was reduced to just over half of what it had been at the age of 17.

8

Changes in occupational status between the ages of 17 and 22 in the light of scholastic ability

When the kind of work in which the men were engaged at the age of 22 is compared with the work in which they had been engaged at 17 in the light of their scholastic ability as assessed when they left school, it is possible to see how far the promise of the 17-year-old was still being maintained in the performance of the 22-year-old. Table 18 summarizes the position for lads who had returned from National Service.

TABLE 18

Three hundred and fifteen men returned from National Service: proportion (as a percentage) of men engaged in various types of work at age 17 and at age 22, classified according to their level of scholastic ability on leaving school

Scholastic assessment on leaving school	Nature of work									
	Skilled manual		Semi-skilled		Unskilled manual		Non-manual		Unemployed	
	At age 17	At age 22	At age 17	At age 22	At age 17	At age 22	At age 17	At age 22	At age 17	At age 22
'A', 'B' (36) (good) .	33·5	30·5	8·5	25	19	25	39	19·5	..	..
'C' (143) (average) .	31·5	24	13	30	25	24	29·5	19	1	3
'D', 'E' (136) (poor) .	35	22	12·5	34	31·5	34	21	10	..	..

One of the striking points that emerges is the heavy fall in the proportion of young men engaged in skilled manual work between the ages of 17 (as apprentices) and 22. This fall affected men of average scholastic ability and, even more heavily, men of poor scholastic quality. The proportion of men engaged in semi-skilled manual work increased remarkably over the period of 5 years, the increase involving men of all degrees of scholastic ability. In general, the proportion of men who were employed as unskilled manual labourers tended to increase slightly over the 5 years; but the number of men engaged in non-manual work fell very considerably. This fact, affecting men of all levels of scholastic ability, was largely a 'growing away from' non-manual jobs of junior clerical and distributive kinds which normally employ a high proportion of young people.

The position among the men rejected as unfit for National Service is set out in Table 19. The proportion of men employed in skilled manual work increased between the ages of 17 and 22 among the few men of above-average scholastic ability; it was just about maintained among those of average ability, but it fell heavily among those of poor scholastic quality. The proportion of men engaged in semi-skilled work increased greatly over the 5 years at all levels of scholastic ability. There was a substantial fall in the proportion of men

TABLE 19

Two hundred and twenty-two men rejected on medical grounds as unfit for National Service: proportion (as a percentage) of men engaged in various types of work at age 17 and at age 22, classified according to their level of scholastic ability on leaving school

Scholastic assessment on leaving school	Nature of work									
	Skilled manual		Semi-skilled		Unskilled manual		Non-manual		Unemployed	
	At age 17	At age 22	At age 17	At age 22	At age 17	At age 22	At age 17	At age 22	At age 17	At age 22
'A', 'B' (13) (good) .	23	38·5	8	38·5	38	8	31	15	..	..
'C' (86) (average) .	23	21	10	26·5	40	36	27	11·5	1	5
'D', 'E' (121) (poor) .	28	14	8	16	36	50	27	12	1	8

of above-average scholastic ability doing unskilled manual labour, as compared with the position 5 years earlier, but a substantial increase in the proportion of men of poor scholastic ability doing unskilled manual work. At all levels of scholastic ability there was a marked fall in the number of men engaged in non-manual work.

9

Apprentices who became skilled workers

The 222 men who were rejected as unfit for National Service included 58 who had been apprentices at the age of 17. Fifteen of them abandoned their apprenticeships before reaching the age of 20, but 9 additional lads later embarked on apprenticeships. By the time the men were 20 years of age, this 'rejected' group therefore included 52 skilled men, 10 of whom had by then completed their period of training.

Between the ages of 20 and 22, 6 more of the original apprentices lapsed (or did not continue at the end of their training in the work in which they had been trained), as did 3 of those who had started their apprenticeships later. By the time they were 22, the 222 men rejected as unfit for Service included 43 skilled workers, 4 of whom were working in non-manual work in which they had undergone a period of training.

Of the 68 men who rendered their National Service in the Royal Air Force, 21 had been apprentices at the age of 17. Two of them abandoned their apprenticeships before going on National Service and 3 at the end of Service, so that 5 abandoned apprenticeships between the ages of 17 and 20. During that period 7 other lads in the group started apprenticeships—5 in their 18th year and 2 at the end of Service. By the time the men were 20, there were 23 skilled or potentially skilled workers among them (one of whom had completed his period of training), an increase of 2 as compared with the number of apprentices at the age of 17. Between the ages of 20 and 22, 5 of the men abandoned their apprenticeships—one of the original apprentices, 3 who had started apprenticeships in their 18th year, and one who had started an apprenticeship on return from National Service; so that at the age of 22 there were 17 skilled or potentially skilled men among those who had served in the Royal Air Force, including one who was working in non-manual work in which he had undergone a period of training.

Of the three men who did their Service in the Royal Navy, two had been apprentices at the age of 17; one of these lapsed before the age of 20, the other was employed in skilled manual work at the age of 22.

Among the 244 men who did their National Service in the Army, 82 had been apprentices at the age of 17. Twenty-eight abandoned their apprenticeships either during the year before going on Service or at the end of Service; but during that period 24 other lads in the group started apprenticeships, either in their 18th year or at the end of Service, so that at the age of 20 there were among those who had served in the Army 78 skilled or potentially skilled men, 9 of whom had completed their period of training, a decrease of 4 as compared with the position at the age of 17. Between the ages of 20 and 22, 21 of the men abandoned the apprenticeship or period of training in which they had embarked, or were not working as trained at the end of the study. This number included 8 of those who had started their training before the age of 17. By the time the men were 22, there were 59 skilled workers in the Army group, including 2 who were doing non-manual work of the kind in which they had been trained.

10

The number of men employed in skilled work at the ages of 17, 20, and 22 years

The position may be summarized thus. Of the 222 men rejected on medical grounds as unfit for National Service:

58 had been serving apprenticeships or undergoing periods of training at the age of 17;

52 were serving apprenticeships or undergoing periods of training at the age of 20;

43 were in skilled work at age 22, 4 of whom were then working in non-manual work in which they had undergone a period of training.

Of the 315 men who were called up and completed the ordinary 2-year period of National Service:

105 had been serving apprenticeships or undergoing periods of training at the age of 17;

102 were serving apprenticeships or undergoing periods of training at the age of 20;

76 were in skilled work at the age of 22, 3 of whom were then working in non-manual work in which they had undergone a period of training.

11

The progress of apprentices in relation to their scholastic ability

These trends in occupational status at the ages of 17 and 22 will be further examined later (Chapter 7) to compare the performance of lads returned from Service with that of lads who, having been rejected as unfit for Service, remained throughout in civil life. But for the present it should be noted that altogether, among the 537 boys included in the study (222 rejected as unfit for Service and 315 who completed 2 years of Service), there were 163 (105 among those called up and 58 among those rejected as unfit) who had been serving apprenticeships, or undergoing periods of training, at the age of

17, apart from 32 who had already, before reaching the age of 17, abandoned apprenticeships on which they had embarked. At the age of 22, 62 of the 105 (59 per cent.) who had been called up for National Service were employed in skilled work, as were 37 of the 58 (64 per cent.) rejected as unfit for National Service. (These figures do not, of course, include those lads who started apprenticeships after the age of 17.)

TABLE 20

Numbers (and percentage) of apprentices at age 17 who were in skilled employment at age 22, in relation to scholastic assessment on leaving school: men called up for Service and medical rejects shown separately

	Called up for Service		Rejected as unfit for Service	
Scholastic assessment on leaving school	*Apprentices at age 17*	*In skilled employment at age 22*	*Apprentices at age 17*	*In skilled employment at age 22*
'A', 'B' (good) . .	13	10 (77%)	3	3
'C' (intermediate) . .	44	29 (66%)	21	15 (71%)
'D', 'E' (poor) . .	48	23 (48%)	34	19 (56%)

Among the lads rejected as unfit for Service the proportion of those who had been serving apprenticeships at the age of 17 who were engaged in skilled work at 22 was higher than among the lads who had been called up for Service. This held at each level of scholastic ability. Taking into account the 32 who had already fallen through an apprenticeship before their seventeenth birthday, it appears that in this series just about 50 per cent. of those who had embarked upon an apprenticeship were in fact working in skilled employment at the age of 22; and that this loss of skill increased rapidly as the level of scholastic ability declined.

12

Nature of employment at the age of 22 in relation to personality assessment on leaving school

The personality assessment of the lads, made by their school teachers when they were about to leave school, was compared with the kind of work in which they were employed at age 22. It was found that of the men rejected as unfit for National Service more than half of those who had been placed in category

'C' (the worst) on personality assessment when they left school were working as unskilled manual labourers at the age of 22, compared with just over a third of those who had been placed in categories 'A' and 'B'. Among those called up for National Service much the same sort of thing held, though at all personality levels the proportion of ex-Servicemen who were working as unskilled manual labourers was lower; of those who had been placed in personality group 'C' (the worst) 40 per cent. were unskilled manual labourers, and of those who had been placed in groups 'A' and 'B', 27 per cent.

13

Nature of employment at the age of 22 in relation to the type of housing district in which the men lived

There was also a degree of correspondence between the type of housing district in which the lads had been living when they left school and the kind of work in which they were engaged at the age of 22. Among the men who were rejected as unfit for National Service, 21 per cent. of those who had been living in 'good' or 'fair' housing districts of older type when they left school were employed in skilled manual work at the age of 22, and 30 per cent. were unskilled labourers: but only 11 per cent. of those who had been living in poor housing districts, or in frank slums, were skilled manual workers at the age of 22, and 55 per cent. were unskilled labourers. The lads who had been living in 'new' local-authority housing areas were following a pattern of employment at the age of 22 which bore no constant relationship to that of the men living in either of the two groups of housing districts of older type.

In both groups—those who had been on National Service and those rejected as unfit—the proportion employed in skilled manual and in non-manual work was higher among those who had lived in good housing districts than among those who had lived in bad; on the other hand, the proportion working as unskilled labourers was higher among those from poor housing districts.

It will be remembered that a similar kind of correspondence was observed (Chapter 4) between the types of housing district in which the men lived at the age of 20 and the kinds of work in which they were employed at the age of 22.

TABLE 21

Proportion (as a percentage) of men engaged in various types of work at age 22, arranged according to the kind of housing district in which they had been living when they left school: men who were subsequently called up for National Service shown separately from men subsequently rejected as unfit for Service

Type of housing district at age 14*	Nature of work at age 22									
	Skilled manual		Semi-skilled		Unskilled manual		Non-manual		Unem-ployed	
	Subsequently did National Service	Subsequently rejected as unfit	Subsequently did National Service	Subsequently rejected as unfit	Subsequently did National Service	Subsequently rejected as unfit	Subsequently did National Service	Subsequently rejected as unfit	Subsequently did National Service	Subsequently rejected as unfit
'New' local-authority (86) (66) . .	21	22	27	15·5	39	40·5	12	14	1	8
Old working-class, 'good' or 'fair' (140) (80) . . .	26	21	29	28	21·5	30	21·5	15	2	6
Old working-class, 'poor' or 'slum' (88) (74) . . .	22	11	39	20	30	55	9	7	..	7

* The figures in brackets in this column indicate the number of men in each housing group who served and who were rejected as unfit for National Service.

14

Change of housing district between the ages of 17 and 22

Parenthetically, it is interesting to observe the change that had come over the type of housing district in which the families of the lads lived between 1947, when the boys were 14 years of age, and 1955, when they were 22 years of age (Table 22).

15

Nature of employment at the age of 22 in relation to father's employment

It has been seen (Chapter 2) that a higher proportion of the lads called up for National Service (especially those serving in the Royal Air Force) were the sons of fathers employed in skilled manual work than was the case with the lads rejected as unfit for National Service. And it is known that in general the sons of skilled fathers have a better prospect of themselves obtaining skilled work.[1]

In this study, the proportion of lads rejected as unfit for Service who were the sons of skilled fathers and were themselves employed on skilled work at the age of 22 was very similar to the corresponding proportion among the ex-Servicemen with skilled fathers. The lads who were rejected as unfit for National

TABLE 22

Change of type of housing district between 1947 and 1955: proportion of families (as a percentage) living in different types of housing district when the lads in this study were aged 14 and 22 years

	Men rejected as unfit for Service		Men called up for Service	
	Percentage of families who lived in this type of district		Percentage of families who lived in this type of district	
Type of housing district in which lad lived	When the lad was 14 years of age	When the lad was 22 years of age	When the lad was 14 years of age	When the lad was 22 years of age
'New' local-authority housing area . . .	30	42	27	41
Old working-class district, 'good' or 'fair' . .	36	33	45	40
Old working-class district, 'poor' or 'slum' . .	34	25	28	19
	100	100	100	100

Service and whose fathers were unemployed or dead when their sons left school at the age of 14 presented quite as good an employment picture at the age of 22 as did the ex-Servicemen whose circumstances were similar.

16

Nature of employment at the age of 22 in relation to lad's job-preference on leaving school

Among the lads rejected as unfit for National Service 25 per cent. of those who had expressed a desire for skilled manual work when they left school were employed in such work at the age of 22; but 34 per cent. of them were then working as

[1] *The Young Wage-Earner*, op. cit.

unskilled labourers. Fifty-two per cent. of those who had wanted semi-skilled work were unskilled labourers, as were 41 per cent. of those who had wanted non-manual work and 51 per cent. of those who had had no job-preference when they left school.

The position among those who had completed 2 years' National Service was that 27 per cent. of those who had desired skilled manual work when they left school were employed in such work at the age of 22, but 25 per cent. of them were then working as unskilled labourers; 36 per cent. of those who had wanted semi-skilled work were then working as unskilled manual workers, as were 5 per cent. of those who had wanted non-manual work, and 20 per cent. of those who had no job-preference when they left school.

When the job-preference of the boys at the age of 14 was set against the kind of job they held at the age of 22, in the light of their scholastic ability, it was found that the proportions of those who had desired skilled manual work on leaving school and had in fact obtained it at the age of 22 scarcely varied as much as might have been expected.

TABLE 23

Proportion (as a percentage) of those who expressed a desire for skilled manual work on leaving school who were in such work at age 22, classified according to level of scholastic ability: men rejected as unfit for National Service shown separately from men who completed 2 years' Service

	Percentage of those who had desired skilled manual work on leaving school who were in such work at age 22	
Scholastic assessment on leaving school	*Men who completed 2 years' Service (315)*	*Men rejected as unfit for National Service (222)*
'A', 'B' (good) . . .	34·8	40·0
'C' (average) . . .	27·3	22·6
'D', 'E' (poor) . . .	24·2	25·6

17

Unemployment

Among the men rejected as unfit for Service, as among those who had completed 2 years' Service, there was a tendency for the amount of unemployment between the ages of 20 and 22 to increase as the level of scholastic ability fell.

18

Earnings

Overall, there was little difference between the wages earned at the age of 22 by men who had completed 2 years' Service and by those who had been rejected, but there was a small group among the rejected men whose wages were lower, perhaps reflecting a degree of physical incapacity. Among the lads who had been placed in groups 'A' or 'B' in point of scholastic ability there was no difference in level of wages at the age of 22 between those who had been on Service and those who had been rejected as unfit, but those rejected for Service who had been placed in groups 'D' or 'E' in point of scholastic ability were receiving slightly lower wages at the age of 22 than those in the same groups who had been on Service.

19

Working time lost from all causes between the ages of 14 and 17, compared with working time lost between the ages of 20 and 22

When the amount of working time lost from all causes during the 3 years between the ages of 14 and 17 was compared with the total working time lost from all causes between the ages of 20 and 22, it emerged that among the men rejected as unfit for National Service those who had lost most time between 14 and 17 also tended to lose most time between 20 and 22, but that, with some exceptions, men who had returned from Service tended to lose less time between 20 and 22, even though they had lost just as much between 14 and 17. Thus, among the 222 men rejected as unfit for National Service there were 65 men who had lost more than 2 months of working time between the ages of 14 and 17; 23 of the 65 also lost more than 2 months of working time between the ages of 20 and 22: among the 315 men returned from National Service 57 had lost more than 2 months of working time between the ages of 14 and 17; 13 of the 57 also lost more than 2 months between the ages of 20 and 22. As was to be expected, the men called up for National Service lost less working time than those rejected as unfit, both between the ages of 14 and 17 and between the ages of 20 and 22.

20

Changes in leisure interests as compared with the 14–17-year age-group

It has been seen (Chapter 4) that the chief leisure interests of the men between the ages of 20 and 22 lay in football, the cinema, and dancing and that the scope of their interests at these ages was wide—much wider than at the age of 17 and inevitably more 'adult' in type. At the age of 17 some 88 per cent. of the lads in the study had been regular cinema fans; in the 20–22-year age-group the figure was about 48 per cent. Membership of an organized social group fell from 36 per cent. at the age of 17 to 11 per cent. in the post-Service period. Only about 25 per cent. of the men attended evening classes at any time between the ages of 14 and 17, but in the 20–22-year age-group this figure was still lower—only 3 or 4 per cent. It was slightly higher among the lads who had not been away on Service; those who were attending evening classes in their twenties were generally the same who had attended earlier.

21

Illustrative cases

It has been seen that about half the lads went more or less uneventfully on their way to a career, whether interrupted by Service or not, following broadly the course that they had already mapped out by the time they were 17 years of age. These are not spectacular cases:

James was the son of a plasterer's labourer. The family—father, mother, and five brothers, of whom James was the eldest—lived in a 'new' three-apartment house in a local-authority housing scheme. The father's employment record was good and the mother was not employed out of the home. The atmosphere of the home was assessed by a social worker as 'good'.

James himself was a well-built lad with a comparatively minor error of refraction. He was a regular school attender, of very good scholastic ability, fond of football and swimming. When he left school his preference was for a semi-skilled trade, but the juvenile advisory committee thought he was well able to learn a skilled job. During the first 8 months after leaving school he held two stop-gap jobs; then his father found for him an apprenticeship with the plasterer with whom he himself was employed. James was still in his apprenticeship when he went on Service to the Army, where his duties, of a 'military' nature, took him overseas; he was made a lance corporal. On return to civil life he went back to complete his apprenticeship, having still 18 months to do; at the end of that period he was retained by his employers as a journeyman plaster at a wage of £9. 10s. a week, plus overtime. He had no unemployment. At the end of 1953 he married and he and his wife went to live in lodgings.

Sometimes the measure of success attained was quite remarkable considering the very bad start in life which many of these young people had:

Andrew lived with his parents, a brother, and a sister, in a single-apartment house in a slum district. The father was a labourer of poor employment record, and the home background was described as reasonably 'good'. Andrew was a likeable lad, though not a great scholar. When he left school he hankered after skilled employment, but the general view was that he was better suited to some repetitive semi-skilled job. For nearly 2 years after leaving school he worked as a store boy in a shoe factory; then he found for himself a job as a labourer in a ship-building yard, and a few months later he was accepted as an apprentice engineer in the same yard. He was called up for National Service at the age of 18 and did not seek deferment, perhaps because conditions at home had deteriorated and he was not very happy there. He went overseas for part of the time he was in the Army and quite enjoyed his Service experience. When he was demobilized he went back to the shipyard to complete his apprenticeship, though receiving little encouragement at home to do so, and he was still an apprentice at the end of the study. About a year after return to civil life he married, and managed to obtain a house of his own, though in a slum district.

George was boarded out with a foster-mother who lived in a three-apartment tenement house in a 'fair' working-class district. His father, who is a cable layer, and his mother live elsewhere; the boy has been living with his present guardian since the age of 9. When he left school at 14 years of age George was 56 inches in height and weighed 80 lb.; his nutrition and general physique were described as 'fair'. Scholastically he was of average ability, though 'poor at figures'. He expressed a preference for skilled manual work, because of its greater interest, but his teacher and the juvenile advisory committee both thought he was better suited to semi-skilled work. After 10 months spent as an errand-boy in a shipyard, he found for himself a job as a trainee waiter in a city hotel. He persevered with his training and, rejected as unfit for National Service because of chronic middle-ear disease, was earning about

£7 a week by the time he was 20 years of age. In due course he became a wine-waiter in the same hotel and at the age of 22 was earning £10 a week 'and upwards', apparently well satisfied with his job and firmly established in it. His leisure interests were wireless, cycling, and reading.

But often it happened that the weight of adverse circumstances was so heavy that, not surprisingly, the lad drifted into the perilous insecurity of casual unskilled labour:

Robert lived in a four-roomed tenement house in a poor work-ing-class district. His father had a shoe-repairing business of his own, but the mother had left the home just before Robert was due to leave school, and the boy's first few weeks after leaving were spent in minding the younger children, of whom there were four. At that time Robert was described as a sad, old-fashioned kind of lad; he was very anxious to get a job as a stable boy, with a view to becoming a jockey, for he loved horses and the country. He was small, poorly nourished, with defective hearing and indifferent vision, a poorish scholar whose attendance at school had been badly inter-rupted by bad health and domestic crises. When he did start work, some 6 weeks after leaving school, it was as a message-boy. After several such jobs he became an apprentice baker, but he was not particularly happy in this job, or with his workmates. His leisure interests were in hiking, football, and badminton. He was rejected as unfit for National Service because of his deafness; and about that time he abandoned his apprenticeship, of which he had served about 2 years. A bad spell followed, with one unpromising job after another, and a good deal of unemployment; at the age of 20, for instance, he had worked for only 1 year of the previous 2 and was then unem-ployed and 'fed up'. Things were almost equally unsatisfactory at home, where there was little happiness; part of the house had been sub-let to another family. Robert became increasingly morose and bad tempered; he was now fond of dancing but annoyed because he could not find a 'steady' girl friend. He said he did not intend to take another job until he got a post which he liked, but at 21 he was working as a shop porter in the city, apparently happier, but now talking of emigrating to Australia. His satisfaction with his job did not last for long; at the end of the study, when 22 years of age, he was working as a pantry boy in a hotel, living in, which he thought would be more interesting.

Tom's father was a motor-driver in a steady job. The family con-sisting of the parents, two boys, and three girls—seven in all—lived in a single-apartment house in a slum area of the city. The assessment of family background was only 'fair'. Tom was described by his school as a poor scholar, irregular in attendance, addicted to truancy, sociable enough, but otherwise not a very good personality. Tom wanted to learn a skilled trade when he left school, but the general consensus of opinion was that he was much more likely to become an unskilled labourer. His jobs were many, at least a dozen in his first 3 years after leaving school; his mother said he had a quick temper and that was why he changed jobs so often. He did his National Service in the Army, partly overseas, and quite enjoyed it, but not to the point of wanting to stay in the Army. On demobilization he went to new work—as a railway shunter—but very soon he left that to become a labourer with the corporation water department. He left that job, in turn, because it offered no scope for overtime and joined the corporation transport department; but, according to his own story, he was dismissed from that job after 4 weeks because of incompetence. Then followed a 6-weeks' spell of unemployment, and at the end of the study he was working as a general labourer.

In 1948 Tom was convicted of attempted house-breaking and admonished; later in the same year he was convicted of theft and placed on probation for 2 years. In 1950 he was convicted of theft and fined £3 with the alternative of 20 days' imprisonment, and in 1954 he was again convicted of theft and of contraventions of the Road Traffic Act; he was fined £10 and had his licence endorsed and suspended for 1 year.

William was the son of a fitter's helper and lived with his parents and three brothers in two rooms of a three-apartment house in a 'new' housing estate; the third room was occupied by a lodger. The mother of the family was very stout and the house very untidy, even dirty. William was a tall, well-built lad, of rather poor scholastic ability, though his school attendance was regular enough; he was described at school as 'hazy' and 'woolly'. On leaving school he expressed a desire to follow a skilled trade and both his teacher and the juvenile advisory committee thought he might make the grade. For 10 months he worked as a van-boy but gave up this work because it carried no prospect of an apprenticeship. Thereafter, for 1 week, he worked on a farm, but the work was too hard and the hours too long. He tried to join the Royal Air Force but was not accepted. Then he found a job as an apprentice electric welder, which he held for 6 months, but he disliked the work and gave it up to become a packer. He, too, was rejected as unfit for National Service because of chronic middle-ear disease. At the age of 20 he was unemployed, having left his work because he disliked it; he had taken to politics and reading. Six months later he was employed as a laundry worker in a hospital; after a further 6 months he was working in the same hospital as a kitchen assistant, and again 6 months later as an assistant cook, this latter job involving residence in the hospital; he was still an ardent politician.

Terence lived with his family in a 'new' local-authority housing estate. The father was dead and the mother out at work: Terence had one brother and two sisters alive, one brother and one sister having died. The general atmosphere of the home was 'poor'. Terence was a very poor scholar, addicted to truancy; and his general personality was described as 'poor'. He expressed a desire for semi-skilled work. When he became eligible for National Service, Terence was still in stop-gap work, but he was very reluctant to go on Service, which he regarded as 'a waste of time'; his mother said he had to be 'lifted' by the Army. When he was demobilized he went to work as a labourer in a steel works; but he was apparently a very irregular worker. A married sister found a lighter job for him but, although he went to it, his employment record continued to be very bad; 'he only works when he feels like it'. His sole interest is gambling and he is constantly pestering his mother for more money to gamble. Terence has few friends and is very much 'agin' society. He was 'difficult' before he enlisted and Service seems to have made him if anything even more so.

Jimmy lived with his mother in a one-apartment tenement house in a poor working-class district. He is an illegitimate child and nothing is known about his father. The home, like the house, is 'poor'. The mother was on public assistance for many years but had recently started to work. Jimmy was described by his mother as 'no very bright' and by his school as frankly 'bad' in scholastic ability; nor was his temperament held in high esteem, except on the score of sociability. He was an undersized boy; his height at 14 was 52½ inches.

Jimmy said he wanted to learn a skilled trade, but everyone else seemed to think he was only fitted for unskilled work. Within 13 months of leaving school Jimmy went through ten jobs, mostly of the message-boy type; but after that he seemed to settle, for over the next 2 years he had only three jobs, all as message-boy. He was fond of cycling and even more fond of the 'pictures' which he attended every night. He professed a mild interest in evening classes, but not to the point of attending any. He was rejected as unfit for National Service, probably because of his poor physique. At the age of 20 he was working as a railway porter, but after 5 weeks he was dismissed from that job as unsuitable. Then followed 5 months of idleness before his next job, as a lamplighter, and when he had been paid off from that he found a resident job as a general worker in an hotel, with a wage of 49*s*. per week, plus full board; but the job was seasonal and, his mother thought, too hard; so he was soon back on unemployment benefit and was still unemployed at the end of the study.

Sometimes it looked as if the lads should have done better than they did:

David was the youngest member of a family of five, of whom all the others were girls. The family lived in a room-and-kitchen house in a good district. The father was a caulker to trade, but was working as a labourer when the boy left school. Home background was described as 'good'. David was a well-built lad of average scholastic ability, a pupil in a junior secondary school. He had no job preference; his teacher and the juvenile advisory committee regarded him as best fitted for semi-skilled work. After a succession of short-term jobs, David became an apprentice joiner in a shipyard but only stayed 9 months in this job because he became annoyed with the foreman and because, in any case, he wanted more money; his chums had more. So he changed his work, became a maker of footballs. Football had always appealed to him and he was a player of some ability. He found his period of Army Service useful in so far as it enabled him to continue his liking for football and his sports training; on demobilization he became a professional footballer. Meanwhile he is doing well enough financially, but a footballer's life is a short one and it would have been better if he had completed his apprenticeship as a joiner.

John's family occupied a fine 'new' five-apartment house in a local-authority housing estate; there were thirteen of them—the parents, three brothers, six sisters, and two relatives—besides John. The father was a labourer, none too regular in work, who became a railway porter; but the home was quite good. John was a good scholar who thought he would like an office job when he left school; the general view was that he was better suited to a skilled manual trade, and he attended a technical college for a year's pre-apprenticeship training. But things did not work out well. He had two jobs as a store-boy with electrical engineering firms, and in due course became an apprentice, though he abandoned his apprenticeship before being called up for National Service. John spent a fair part of his Service time in hospital receiving treatment for a skin condition, and when he returned to civil life he became a barman in a public house. This job did not last long; he gave it up because it was 'too confining' and he remained idle for 4 months, when he

obtained a job as a tram-driver. He was still in this employment at
the end of the study and there seemed to be a reasonable chance that
he would settle down in it.

Both of these lads had already fallen through apprenticeships
before they went on Service. It sometimes happened that a
young man was obviously unsettled by his rejection on the
score of unfitness for National Service, like Jimmy (above) or
Richard:

Richard's parents are living apart, his mother on public assistance; the whereabouts of the father, a labourer, are unknown. The
mother, Richard, and his three brothers, live in a two-apartment
tenement house in a poorish district. The general atmosphere of the
home is described as 'good'. When he left school Richard was undersized—54 inches in height—and of poor physique. At school he was
a regular attender and a fair performer; and when he left he wanted
to learn a trade. His first job on leaving school was in the clothing
trade, apprenticed as a tailor's cutter, and although he changed his
employer on several occasions, generally to a higher wage, he never
departed from his apprenticeship; in the course of 3 years he missed
only 1 month of working time. His leisure interests at this time were
chiefly football, billiards, and golf. To his disgust, he was rejected as
unfit for National Service and thereupon became very unsettled.
He made a short excursion to Manchester, intending to work there
at his trade, but after a week or two in the south he returned to
Glasgow, though still unsettled. He continued to work as a tailor's
cutter, changing his employer from time to time in pursuit of more
money and more experience. By the time he was 21 years of age he
was earning £9 per week and, though he had had about 3 months
of unemployment between the ages of 18 and 22 and was still com-
plaining of being unsettled, he seemed to be pretty well established
as a journeyman in his trade at the end of the study.

6

Crime

Comparison of the incidence of juvenile crime in this study with that in the original series

As already reported elsewhere,[1] 12·2 per cent. of the 1,315 boys included in the earlier basic study (from which the boys covered by the present investigation were drawn) had been convicted in the courts at least once between their 8th and 18th birthdays. Of the 568 boys included in this study—346 who did Service in the Forces (whether for the ordinary period of two years or not) and 222 rejected on medical grounds as unfit for National Service—69 had been convicted at least once between their 8th and 18th birthdays, a figure equal to 12·2 per cent. of the boys at risk, so that the pre-Service rate of delinquency was the same among the boys in this study as among the whole series covered by the original work.

2

Convictions under 18 years of age

Among the 346 men subsequently called up (or volunteering) for National Service at the age of 18, there were 15 who had been convicted between their 8th and 14th birthdays; these 15 lads were convicted altogether 28 times while still at school. Four of the 15 were convicted again between their 14th and 18th birthdays and, in addition, 28 further lads in the group who subsequently went on Service were convicted for the first time between their 14th and 18th birthdays; so that by the time they were 18 years of age 43 of the men (12·4 per cent.) who subsequently went on Service had been convicted in the courts, and their total convictions over the 10 years between their 8th and 18th birthdays numbered 84. The proportion

---

[1] *The Young Delinquent in His Social Setting*, T. Ferguson. Published for the Nuffield Foundation by the Oxford University Press, 1952.

convicted between the ages of 8 and 18 was much lower among the 73 who served in the Royal Air Force than among the 264 who served in the Army, a finding which has to be read along with the fact (Chapter 2) that the lads who subsequently served in the Royal Air Force were drawn, in the main, from better homes than those who served in the Army.

Similarly, among the men who were subsequently rejected as unfit for National Service, there were 14 who had been convicted at least once between their 8th and 14th birthdays; these 14 were convicted altogether 27 times while still at school. Eight of the 14 were convicted again between their 14th and 18th birthdays and, in addition, 13 further lads in the group subsequently rejected as unfit for National Service were convicted for the first time between their 14th and 18th birthdays, so that by the time they were 18 years of age 27 of the men (12·2 per cent.) who were subsequently rejected as unfit for Service had been convicted in the courts, and their total convictions over the 10 years between their 8th and 18th birthdays numbered 55.

The position, therefore, so far as it concerned delinquency before the age of 18, was virtually the same, both in regard to proportion of boys convicted and frequency of convictions, among the 346 men who went on Service and the 222 men rejected as unfit for National Service on medical grounds.

3

Convictions in the 2 years between 18 and 20 years of age

In the 2 years between their 18th and 20th birthdays four of the 346 men who went on Service were convicted in the civil courts for the first time and two who had previously been convicted were again convicted, so that in the course of these 2 years six of the men called up for Service were convicted (each on one occasion only) in the civil courts. It must, of course, be kept in mind that these men were under Service discipline at the time. No record of their Service 'troubles' is available, nor would it necessarily be directly comparable with civilian criminal records, even if it were available; and in considering the proportion of National Servicemen convicted in the civilian courts during the 2 years it has to be remembered that a considerable number of them served overseas for part at least of their Service period.

In the 2 years between their 18th and 20th birthdays two of the 222 men rejected as unfit for National Service were convicted for the first time, and four who had been previously convicted were again convicted, so that in the course of the 2 years six of the 222 men rejected as unfit for National Service had been convicted in the courts; they had among them ten convictions during the 2 years. It does not seem to be useful to speculate on the relative frequency of conviction between the ages of 18 and 20 among the men away on Service during the period and among those who were rejected as unfit for National Service and remained in civil life.

4

Convictions between the ages of 20 and 22

Between the ages of 20 and 22, in their two immediate post-Service years, 14 of the 346 men who had been away (4·0 per cent.) were convicted on at least one occasion, 16 convictions in all; 7 of the 14 convicted in the course of these 2 years were then convicted for the first time. On the other hand, 28 of the 32 lads (87 per cent.) who had been convicted at least once between the ages of 14 and 18 had no further convictions in the course of the 2 years immediately following their return from Service.

Between the ages of 20 and 22, 10 of the 222 men rejected as unfit for National Service (4·5 per cent.) were convicted on at least one occasion, 16 convictions in all; 6 of the 10 convicted in the course of these 2 years were then convicted for the first time. On the other hand, 16 of the 19 lads (84 per cent.) who had been convicted at least once between the ages of 14 and 18 had no further convictions in the course of the 2 years between their 20th and 22nd birthdays.

In the light of these facts it appears to be a reasonable inference that the incidence of crime among men who have performed their National Service between the ages of 18 and 20 is virtually the same at ages between 20 and 22 as the incidence of crime during the same period among men who were rejected as unfit for National Service; nor does there appear to be any material difference between those who have been on Service and those remaining in civil life in the proportion of men who, having been convicted between the ages of 14 and 18, have no further convictions between the ages of 20 and 22.

There was little or no difference in the kinds of crime committed between the ages of 20 and 22 by men who had returned from Service to civil life and those who had never been away. Among both groups simple theft accounted for half of the convictions and about a quarter were in respect of housebreaking or attempted house-breaking; the others were a very mixed bag—loitering with intent to steal, stealing motor vehicles, breach of the peace, and other offences. There was only one conviction for a sexual offence (an ex-Serviceman).

5

Number of men convicted at different ages; men called up for Service and men unfit for Service compared

Table 24 analyses by age at conviction the criminal records of men called up for National Service and of men rejected on medical grounds as unfit for Service.

TABLE 24

The number of men convicted before reaching the age of 18, and the number convicted for the first time after that age: men who were away on National Service and men rejected as unfit for Service shown separately

	Total no. in group	No convictions recorded	Convicted between 8th and 18th birthdays but not later	Convicted for first time after 18th birthday	Convicted both before and after 18th birthday
Men who undertook National Service	346	292	37	11	6
Men rejected as unfit for National Service	222	187	21	8	6

6

The social and economic background of the men convicted

The incidence of convictions in the several age-groups has been set against certain available information about the social and environmental history of the men concerned—the assessment of scholastic ability, as made by their school teachers when they left school; the home assessment, made by an experienced social visitor about the same time; the kind of housing district in which they were then living; the kind of job in which the lads were employed at the age of 18 and at the age of 22; and the amount of unemployment they experienced between the ages of 20 and 22.

The relationship between the proportion of men convicted and their social and environmental background is in general agreement with that already described elsewhere.[1] Thus, considering all the men included in the study—whether called up for National Service or rejected as unfit—the proportion convicted rose steeply as the level of scholastic ability declined. Those who came from 'good' homes had a lower conviction rate than those whose homes were only 'fair' or 'bad'. Those who lived in 'good' or 'fair' housing districts of older type had only about half the conviction rate of those who lived in 'poor' or 'slum' areas; those who lived in 'new' local-authority housing schemes fell between these two extremes, doubtless because of the very wide range of families to be found in the new districts. There was a measure of correspondence between the proportion of men convicted and the nature of the work in which they were employed: those in skilled manual work, for example, had fewer convictions than those who were unskilled labourers. The proportion of men convicted rose rapidly with the amount of unemployment experienced between the 2 years of the study; among those men who had lost no working time through unemployment in the course of the 2 years, 11 per cent. had been convicted, but among those who had lost over 2 months' working time 30 per cent. had been convicted.

The relationship between the proportion of men convicted and social and environmental factors was not uniformly even in the two series of men—those who had been away on Service and those rejected as unfit—though there was a reasonable measure of correspondence. The number of men 'at risk' is too small to permit an extensive analysis. The two chief differences were, first, that the men rejected as unfit for National Service did not show the same clear relationship between the proportion

---

[1] *The Young Delinquent in His Social Setting*, op. cit.

convicted and the nature of the occupation in which they had
been employed at the age of 17, although the relationship with
the occupation in which they were employed at the age of 22
was clear enough; and, second, that the proportion convicted
bore no striking relationship to scholastic ability, as assessed by
their teachers when they left school.

Table 25 summarizes the relationship between the proportion
of men convicted at least once between the ages of 8 and 22 and
these various social and environmental factors.

TABLE 25

*Proportion (as a percentage) of men known to have been convicted at least
once between the ages of 8 and 22 in relation to certain social and
environmental factors: men who were called up for National Service
shown separately from men rejected as unfit for Service*

| | | | Percentage of men convicted | | |
	Social and environmental factors*		Served for 2 years	Rejected as unfit for Service	Both series together
Scholastic assessment	'A', 'B' (good)	(36) (13)	6	15	8
	'C' (average)	(143) (86)	13	17	14
	'D', 'E' (poor)	(136) (121)	20	15	18
Home assessment	'Good'	(227) (157)	13	15	14
	'Fair' or 'Bad'	(88) (62)	20	19	20
Type of housing district	'New' local authority	(86) (66)	14	15	14
	Old, good or fair	(140) (80)	11	12·5	11
	Old, poor or slum	(98) (74)	20	20	20
Occupational status at age 17	Skilled, manual	(105) (58)	11	14	12
	Semi-skilled	(38) (20)	16	20	17
	Unskilled	(79) (85)	20	13	16·5
	Non-manual	(82) (57)	16	21	18
Occupational status at age 22	Skilled, manual	(73) (39)	16	10	14
	Semi-skilled	(93) (47)	17	13	16·5
	Unskilled	(86) (92)	19	22	22
	Non-manual	(46) (26)	4	8	5·5
Unemployment (weeks) between 20 and 22 years of age	None	(187) (135)	11	11	11
	1–8	(67) (50)	19	16	18
	9+	(46) (32)	28	31	30

* The numbers in brackets in this column refer to the number of men in each group who
served for 2 years and to the number rejected as unfit.

It will be observed that in relation to such basic and environmental factors as the quality of the home and the type of
district in which the men lived as well as in relation to scholastic
ability there is a tendency for the difference in proportions
convicted between the good and bad ends of the scale to be

wider among the men who were away on Service than among those rejected as unfit for Service.

7

Illustrative cases

Henry's father was a plasterer who had experienced a fair amount of unemployment; he had a small war pension for a wound sustained in the First World War. Henry's mother went out to work. The family consisted of five sisters and Henry, who had been third of seven (one dead); but in addition there were four lodgers in the four-roomed tenement house, making twelve persons in all. The family atmosphere was described as 'good' by an experienced social worker.

Henry was a cyclist, also interested in football, jazz, and 'pictures', with a special fondness for 'crime' films. He was an undersized boy, $52\frac{1}{2}$ inches in height and weighing 77 lb. when he left school at the age of 14. He was a poor scholar, irregular in attendance, and given to truancy. When he left school he wanted to be a carpenter, but after four or five short-term jobs of the message-boy type, his father got him apprenticed to a firm of slaters. He soon fell through his apprenticeship and turned to general labouring work, with a good deal of unemployment. He was rejected as unfit for National Service; according to himself, because of a perforated ear-drum.

Between the ages of 20 and 22 Henry worked mostly with the cleansing department, when he was at work; but in the course of the 2 years he had some 35 weeks of unemployment. Meanwhile the family had moved to a two-roomed house in which there were sometimes as many as ten occupants.

At the age of 11 Henry was convicted of theft by house-breaking (two charges) and placed on probation. At the age of 14 he was found guilty of house-breaking with intent to steal and placed on probation for a period of 2 years. At the age of 18 he was convicted of theft by house-breaking and fined £5 with the alternative of 30 days' imprisonment; and again a year later he received a similar sentence for theft by house-breaking. Then, when 21 years of age, he was sent to prison for 4 months on two charges of theft and contravention of the Road Traffic Act.

Howard's father and mother have been separated since he was 3 years old. The father is an unskilled labourer (navvy), often working away from home, and the boy and his sisters are looked after by their grandmother in a slum tenement room-and-kitchen house. Apart from football, Howard had no leisure interests; he liked to be with 'the boys'.

Howard was an undersized, undernourished lad, 52 inches in

height and 60 lb. in weight when he left school. He was a fair scholar, a regular attender at school, and when he left school he wanted to learn a trade. But, like so many others of similar background, he could not get an apprenticeship and moved uneasily from one stop-gap job to another. By the time he was 17 years of age he had had more than half a dozen such jobs, and fully 3 months of unemployment. He was rejected as unfit for National Service, being placed in grade IV, and shortly after he, too, obtained a job in the corporation cleansing department where he continued to work fairly steadily for some years though, according to his grandmother, he was always a very 'difficult' boy.

Howard's criminal record commenced at the age of 13, when he was admonished for theft. Between the ages of 15 and 21 he had at least one conviction every year—in 1948 and 1949, for theft; in 1950 and 1951 for house-breaking and again in 1951 for loitering with intent to steal, being a known thief; in 1952 for assault and again for house-breaking; in 1953 for loitering with intent to steal, being a known thief; and in 1954 for theft.

In both of these cases the criminal record was long and the physical environment bad; neither went on Service, but it is hard to believe that, even if they had served, it would have made any real difference to the career on which both are only too clearly embarked. Peter had a similar environment and a similar record. He was on Service, but it is equally difficult to believe that his period of Service influenced the pattern of his career in any substantial way.

Peter lived with his mother, three brothers, and a sister in a room-and-kitchen in a tenement in the east end of the city. His father was dead: his mother was out at work, but the general atmosphere of the home was described as 'quite good'. Peter was a well-built lad, a fair scholar in a junior secondary school: he himself wanted a semi-skilled job when he left school, but the juvenile advisory committee thought he should be fit for a skilled trade. He was, in fact, apprenticed to a chairmaker at the age of 15, after a short spell as an errand-boy, and he continued in his apprenticeship—when he was available for work—until called up for National Service in March 1951. Part of his time on Service was spent in Japan; he liked his Service days and liked being overseas. He was demobilized in March 1953, and a week late resumed his apprenticeship as a chairmaker, with a weekly wage of £7. 13s. He had no difficulty in settling back into civil life; at that time he described his leisure interests as football, 'pictures', and the theatre. He remained continuously in the employment of the same firm throughout the 2 years of this study.

Peter's criminal record goes back to 1945, while he was still at school: he was convicted of house-breaking with intent to steal and was placed on probation for 1 year. A few months after leaving school in 1947 he appeared in a London court as a young person in need of care and attention and was the subject of a supervision order for 1 year. But the following month he was back in Glasgow, again charged with attempted house-breaking, and his mother was fined. In 1948 he had five separate convictions—in February for theft (admonished) and again in the same month for theft (14 days' detention). Four months later he was convicted of theft and theft by house-breaking (28 days' detention) and again 2 months later, theft (28 days' detention). In November 1948 there was another sentence of 28 days' detention for being a known thief found loitering with intent to steal. In 1949 he was sentenced to 3 months' imprisonment for theft and the following year, a suspected person loitering with intent to steal, he was sent for Borstal training. Seven months later he was called up for Military Service and on demobilization returned to Glasgow—and chair-making. Not until the following year did he next appear in court, again for theft, to be sentenced to 60 days' imprisonment.

Joseph lived with his parents, five sisters, and a lodger in a three-apartment house in a local-authority housing estate. His father was an unskilled labourer with a bad employment record. The general assessment of the family was only 'fair'. Joseph's interests were in football and in reading crime stories. He was a smallish boy, 54 inches in height on leaving school, but quite well nourished. As a scholar Joseph was very poor, irregular in attendance at school and addicted to truancy, and the height of his ambition on leaving school was to get an unskilled labouring job. Actually he went through an almost uncountable number of such jobs, with, however, very little unemployment between the ages of 14 and 18. He was rejected as unfit for National Service (discharging ear), and following his rejection he did not work at all for a period of nearly 3 years, though towards the end of that period he got married and was soon living with his wife and baby in a sub-let room in a poor tenement house. He started work again in January 1954 as a labourer in a cement works but was dismissed in June, and after that he found another labouring job in which he was still employed at the end of this study.

Rather surprisingly, Joseph had no convictions while still at school, but within 3 months of leaving he was convicted of theft by house-breaking, his father being fined £2 caution for his son's good behaviour for 12 months. Five years later, in 1952, he had two separate convictions for theft. In 1953 he was again convicted on two charges of theft and in 1955 he was sent to prison for 60 days after another conviction for theft.

Michael, the son of a labourer, lived with his parents, two brothers, and two sisters in a 'fair' old two-room-and-kitchen house. His father's employment record was good; the mother was not employed out of the home, which was clean and tidy. Michael was of average height and physique, but though regular in school attendance he was a very poor scholar. He did not know what kind of work he wanted when he left school; in the view of his teacher and the juvenile advisory committee he was most likely to become an unskilled labourer. Between the ages of 14 and 17 he held seven jobs of labouring or messenger type, and he was working as a labourer in an engineering works when he volunteered for Army Service late in 1952, a month or two ahead of his 18th birthday. He served as a motor driver in the Royal Artillery, part of the time in Germany, and on return to civil life worked for a few months on a construction scheme in the country. Then he returned to his old job as a labourer in an engineering works in Glasgow and continued in that work throughout the 2 years of the study: but during this period he had fully 3 months of unemployment. He married early in 1954 and took his wife to live with his own family, who by that time had moved to a three-apartment local-authority 'slum clearance' house.

Michael's first conviction—for theft—was recorded when he was 16 years of age; he was admonished. The following year, before going on Service, he was again convicted of theft and fined £2 with the alternative of 20 days' imprisonment. Shortly after demobilization, while working away from Glasgow on the construction scheme, he was again convicted of theft and sentenced to 1 month's imprisonment, and 2 months later, after his return to the city, he was convicted of house-breaking and placed on probation for 2 years: since then there has been no further trouble.

Michael and Joseph had a good deal in common. Both had an overcrowded tenement background; both were poor scholars; both kept moving aimlessly from job to job between the ages of 14 and 17; both took to crime after leaving school. One was on Service, the other not, but both continued in crime at post-Service ages.

Alexander's father is dead; the lad lives in a room-and-kitchen tenement house with his mother and his sister. The home is reasonably good, though the mother is out at work. Alexander was quite a sturdy youngster, a moderate pupil in a junior secondary school. When he left school he wanted to learn a skilled trade, and the general opinion was that he had enough capacity to do so. His first job was as a van-boy with a baker, apparently with the idea of going on to an apprenticeship in that trade; but instead he took up an engineering apprenticeship in a foundry. He continued in that work until he was called up for National Service in the Army. Part of his Service was overseas, driving a tank. When he was demobilized, in February 1953, he returned not to foundry work but to his old love as a baker, taking up an apprenticeship in that trade. He continued to work as a baker throughout the 2 years of the study, with one change of employer.

Alexander kept out of police trouble while at school; indeed, his first conviction was not until April 1951, by which time he had joined the Army; he was admonished for theft. In October 1953, 6 months after discharge from Service, he was again convicted of theft and placed on probation for 2 years; and 4 months later he was again convicted of theft and sentenced to 2 months' imprisonment.

Hector's father was dead and the boy lived with his mother, five brothers, and one sister—eight in all—in a room-and-kitchen tenement house. The mother was in indifferent health and the family background was only 'fair'. Hector was of fair physique, though he had lost a considerable amount of schooling through minor illness. He was described as of average scholastic ability and wanted to learn a skilled trade, which seemed to be within his capacity. For eighteen months after leaving school he worked as a grocer's boy, and then found for himself an apprenticeship with a painter in which he continued until called up for Army Service. Part of his Service was spent overseas; he, too, drove a tank. He quite liked Service life and experienced some difficulty in settling back as a civilian, chiefly because he had left a girl friend in England. He did not go back to his apprenticeship as a painter, but on demobilization started work as a labourer in an engineering works at a wage of 95s. per week. He remained in this work for a year, then left because it offered no prospects. A long spell of unemployment followed—some 9 months in all—before he found an unskilled job in a Royal Ordnance factory, but he was only 3 months in this job when he was dismissed for stealing metal.

Hector steered clear of police trouble until January 1952 when he was still on Service. He was then convicted in Glasgow of house-breaking, presumably when on leave; sentence was deferred and no further order made. Then, in November 1953, came the conviction for theft of metal mentioned above; he was sentenced to 30 days' imprisonment.

Hector and Alexander were both on Service and both had clean records until they went on Service; both had further convictions after they returned to civil life. It would be easy to blame their turn to crime on the fact that they were on Service—and indeed Service may have played a large part in it—but consider the case of Reginald who, too, had no convictions until he was 20 years of age and then took to crime although he was not away on Service.

Reginald lived with his parents, three sisters, and two brothers, eight in all, in a single room in a very bad slum; an elder sister, 18 years of age, lived with her grandmother because of shortage of room. The house was in a shocking state of dirt and disorder, squalor everywhere. Yet when the home was first visited in the course of the original study the new baby of 6 months sat smiling happily in her dirty pram by the fireside, while two small pre-school children craned at perilous angles out of the open window. The mother assured the visitor that there was no danger. The father, an ex-docker, was then employed as a general labourer in a sweet factory; his employment record is described as 'fair'.

Reginald is himself a lad of quite good physique, of reasonable competence at school, above average in handicrafts, but irregular in attendance and inclined to truancy. He plays football and likes to listen on the wireless to dance bands and Dick Barton. He is a keen member of a youth club but, above all, he likes horses and motors and, not surprisingly, wanted to be a van-boy when he left school. Instead, he went to work in a foundry, soldering pipes, and was ultimately accepted as an apprentice pipe-dresser. He was rejected as unfit for Service, but he thereupon gave up his pipe-dressing apprenticeship and became an apprentice baker. When he was 20 years of age he was paid off from his baking apprenticeship and went to work as a labourer on road-repair schemes. The last information available about him at his home was that he had gone to work in London where the nature of his work was unknown. He soon returned to Glasgow, as his criminal record shows.

Reginald had no convictions until he was 20 years of age, when he was found guilty of house-breaking and fined £15 with the alternative of 60 days' imprisonment; it was about this time that he was paid off from his baking apprenticeship. Nearly a year later, in January 1953, he was found guilty of a contravention of section 28 of the Road Traffic Act; and there was another conviction the following month. In January 1955 he was convicted of attempted house-breaking and fined £15 with the alternative of 60 days' imprisonment.

7
Summary

I

The scope of the work

THIS study is concerned primarily with the performance over a
period of 2 years, while they were between the ages of 20 and
22, of 568 men about whose earlier history much information
happened to be available from an investigation carried out
during the 3 years 1947–50, immediately after the lads left
school at the earliest permitted age, then 14 years.[1]

The lives of young men in their early twenties are often
highly coloured by the impact of National Service, and any
study of men of this age must inevitably be largely bound up
with consideration of the effects of Service. Indeed, in planning
this work, it was found to be convenient to confine its scope to
two groups of men, one consisting of 346 who had done their
National Service and returned to civil life by the time they were
20 years of age, the other consisting of 222 of similar age who
had been rejected on medical grounds as unfit for Service and
had remained in civil life in Glasgow since they left school. The
study was limited to these two groups chiefly because the inclu-
sion of the others of the same age-group for whom information
was available—such as those whose period of National Service
was deferred to enable them to complete an apprenticeship or
period of training—would have prolonged the investigation
over a period of years long enough to create major new difficulties of comparability and interpretation.

It would have been satisfactory if it had been possible to
include in the present study all the lads in the two groups
selected—those who later went on Service and those rejected as
unfit—who had been included in the earlier study of school-
leavers; but for a variety of reasons this could not be done.
The present study embraces about 76 per cent. of the lads included in *The Young Wage-Earner* investigation who were called
up for National Service on—or very shortly after—reaching the

[1] *The Young Wage-Earner*, op. cit.

age of 18 years, and 84 per cent. of those rejected as unfit for National Service. There is no reason to believe that the experience of these young men is not fairly typical of the groups to which they belonged.

It is not easy to assess the effects of Service on the lives of young people. There can be little doubt that in some cases impending Service affects the attitude to their future career of the lads concerned and their parents; no study such as this can hope to measure these effects, if indeed they are measurable. Even where it is possible to use certain indexes that are available to measure the subsequent performance of those who have been away against the performance of those who have not, many potential fallacies have to be kept in mind. For one thing, there is the effect on a lad of the mere fact that he has been rejected for Service; we have seen cases where rejection unsettled the lad and seemed to make him 'difficult'. Again, a certain proportion, though by no means all, of the lads rejected as unfit must have suffered in earlier days from the restraints of illness or the loss of schooling that goes with it, or been left with a degree of disability, sometimes a handicap to employment. Further, it is known that about one-third of those who went on Service at the age of 18 had been serving apprenticeships at the age of 17, when the earlier study ended; and since it is open to apprentices to apply for deferment of National Service to enable them to complete their apprenticeships, it is probably a reasonable assumption that some, at least, of the apprentices who chose to go on Service at the age of 18 did so because they were already unsettled, or not getting on very well in their apprenticeships. In addition, there are fundamental issues of social and environmental background—level of scholastic ability, for example, or the kind of home from which the lads are drawn—clearly matters that are likely to influence profoundly subsequent performance. Experience has shown that it is often difficult to assemble groups of lads who are reasonably comparable in these important matters.

2

Available information

Arising from our earlier work, we were fortunate in having, for each of the lads in this study, a full range of assessments made independently by physicians and teachers at the time the boy left school—information about height, general physique, personality, regularity of school attendance, and standard of scholastic ability. A study of these assessments, made when the boys were 14 years of age, showed that, as a group, those who embarked on National Service at or very soon after their 18th birthday approximated reasonably closely to, or fell not far short of, the average performance of Glasgow school-leavers of their age; but that the boys rejected as unfit for National Service cut altogether poorer figures.

Similarly, records were available about the home background of each lad and about his working experience between the ages of 14 and 17. Concerning home background, information was available about the kind of district in which the lads lived, size of family, severity of crowding in the home, nature of the father's employment, and the regularity of that employment; and there was available an assessment of the general family background, made by an experienced social worker. In regard to the employment record of the lads between the ages of 14 and 17, information was available about the kind of job each boy had desired when he left school, the number and kinds of job he held in the course of the 3 years, whether he embarked on any apprenticeships during that period, the amount of time lost through illness or unemployment; and, in particular, the type of work in which the lad was engaged at the age of 17, and his attitude to it—whether he regarded it as the kind of work in which he would like to continue or merely as a stop-gap. The differences in these matters between the lads called up for Service and those rejected as unfit were rather less clear-cut than the differences in the range of assessments made at the time of school-leaving; but in general the boys who went on Service at the age of 18 fell not far short of the average performance of the other boys of their age who had left school at the same time whereas the boys rejected as unfit for Service had a much poorer record: they hailed from poorer districts, a higher proportion were the sons of unskilled labourers, and they had shown—between the ages of 14 and 17—a much poorer standard of performance at work.

The men who did their Service in the Royal Air Force had enjoyed, at home, considerable environmental advantages over those who served in the Army, and their general standard of performance before going on Service, both at home and at work, had been better.

This information about the earlier background of the lads is obviously of great importance in seeking to compare the later performance of one group with another. Apart from any influence, for good or ill, which the period of National Service may have had on subsequent careers, it would scarcely be reasonable, in view of their past history, to expect the lads rejected as unfit for National Service to do as well in later years as the lads called up for Service.

3

Glasgow boys compared with other National Servicemen

The national figures show a lower proportion of rejections on medical grounds than that experienced among the Glasgow boys embraced in this study. Among the Glasgow lads the chief causes of rejection appeared to be, in order, deafness and associated ear conditions, visual defects, and lung conditions, including pulmonary tuberculosis. On entry to the Army, these Glasgow boys contained relatively too many who were classified in grade II as compared with grade I; but by the time the men were released from Service, the proportions were roughly the same as those for the whole country.

These Glasgow boys were, on average, shorter and lighter than other National Servicemen when they were called up, the weight difference being accounted for mainly by the difference in height. Their gain in weight while on Service was substantial, but left the boys in this study, as compared with the 'control' group, in relatively the same position on release from Service as they had been on entry to it. In general, the boys who were taller on leaving school were also taller in the Army, and the boys who were heavier on leaving school were also heavier in the Army.

4

Service experience of men called up for National Service

One hundred and ninety-seven of the 315 men who completed 2 years' National Service served overseas for some part of the time, the principal overseas theatre of Service being the Far East. Fifty-five of the 315 reported that while on Service they had received training in a trade, and 14 of them said that this Service training had counted towards a civilian apprenticeship. Fifty-one of the 315 claimed to have received promotion to N.C.O. rank while on Service; the lads promoted were, in general, taller and had, at the time of leaving school, a better level of personality assessment than the others. Of men who had been placed in groups 'A' or 'B' (at the better end of the scale) in point of scholastic ability when they left school 14 per cent. had been promoted; of those in group 'C' 21 per cent.; and of those in groups 'D' or 'E' (at the bad end of the scale) 12 per cent. The proportion promoted was higher among men who had been engaged in semi-skilled work before being called up for National Service (24 per cent.) than among those who had been serving an apprenticeship (16 per cent.), or done non-manual work (18 per cent.), or been unskilled manual labourers (11 per cent.).

Fifty-eight per cent. of those who completed 2 years' National Service reported on return to civil life that they had enjoyed their Service experience, 18 per cent. that they had disliked it, while 24 per cent. were neutral, regarding it, for the most part, 'as just a job that had to be done'. Only 7 per cent. expressed a preference for Service life as compared with civil life. Posting overseas did not appear greatly to affect liking for Service life. There was a tendency for those who expressed dislike for Service to include more than a fair share of lads of low scholastic ability and a relatively high proportion living in 'new' local-authority housing schemes.

5

Settling into civil life after return from Service

Fully two-thirds of those who had been on Service went back to work within 1 month of their return to civil life; 6 per cent. had not yet started work 2 months after return. Sixty-two per cent. of the men went back to their pre-Service job; the proportion was higher (73 per cent.) among those who had served in the Royal Air Force than among those who had served in the Army (59 per cent.). Some 28 per cent. of the men demobilized returned to their old jobs intending to complete apprenticeships which they had interrupted to go on Service.

Twenty-one per cent. of the men who had been away on National Service experienced some difficulty in settling back into civil life. Their difficulties were usually associated with employment—either dislike of the job itself or of the wages that went with it. Sometimes difficulties were of a domestic nature, sometimes they turned on adaptation to the altered values implicit in a return to civil life. As was to be expected, the proportion of men who reported difficulty in settling was lower among those who had returned to their pre-Service jobs.

6

Employment status between the ages of 20 and 22

At the age of 20, 32·5 per cent. of the men who had been on National Service for 2 years were employed in skilled manual work, and 19·1 per cent. in semi-skilled work. At the age of 22 the proportion in skilled work had fallen to 24·1 per cent., while the proportion in semi-skilled work had risen to 30·7 per cent. Over the same period of time the proportion of men rejected as unfit for National Service who were engaged in skilled manual work fell from 23·4 per cent. to 17·9 per cent., and the proportion in semi-skilled work remained constant at 21·6 per cent. Seventy-four per cent. of the men returned from National Service who had been skilled manual workers (or still serving an apprenticeship) at the age of 20 were engaged in skilled manual work (or still serving an apprenticeship) at the age of 22; the corresponding figure among those rejected as unfit for National Service was 76·5 per cent. This decline in the proportion of men employed in skilled work will be considered later in the light of the previous social and environmental background of the men concerned.

There was little difference in gross weekly wage at the age of 22 between those who had been on Service and those rejected as unfit.

7

Working time lost through unemployment and illness

Taken at its face value, time lost through unemployment during the 2 years between the ages of 20 and 22 was very similar in amount whether the men had been called up or rejected as unfit; in both groups, some 62 per cent. lost no working time, while 11 per cent. lost 3 months or more in the course of 2 years. The amount of time lost through unemployment was greater among those who had done their Service in the Army than among those who had served in the Royal Air Force. Unemployment and difficulty in settling back into civil life went hand-in-hand: men who went back to their pre-Service job experienced less unemployment than the others.

But, over the 2 years, the men who had been rejected on medical grounds as unfit for National Service lost much more time through illness than those who had been called up; fewer of them wholly escaped sickness incapacity and more of them had long-term sickness absence. In both groups of men prolonged absence on account of illness was most common among those who had been unskilled labourers or unemployed at the age of 20.

It is often difficult to differentiate between unemployment and time lost through illness—the one is apt to run into the other—and it is an interesting finding that where no time was lost through illness in the course of the 2 years between the ages of 20 and 22, 64 per cent. of the men who had been rejected as unfit for Service wholly escaped unemployment, as compared with only 45 per cent. of those who had been called up. Where some time had been lost through illness, on the other hand, 61 per cent. of the men rejected as unfit escaped unemployment, as against 69 per cent. of those who had been on Service: so that, in the absence of illness, unemployment was a good deal more prevalent among the men who had been called up.

8

Frequency of change of job between the ages of 20 and 22

During their first 6 months back in civil life after return from National Service 85 per cent. of the men who had been called up remained in the job which they took up on demobilization, doubtless partly in exercise of 'reinstatement rights'. During the corresponding 6 months only 69 per cent. of the men who had been rejected as unfit remained continuously in the same job. Thereafter the gap between the two groups quickly narrowed and 18 months later, at the age of 22, only 46 per cent. of the men returned from National Service had remained in the same job throughout the period of 2 years, and among those who had been rejected as unfit the proportion without change of job over the same period was almost exactly the same, 45·6 per cent.

9

The influence of social and environmental background on unemployment

Comparisons between one group and the other can be misleading unless considered in the light of the social and environmental background of the men concerned, as a few examples will show.

The extent and severity of unemployment during the 2 years between the ages of 20 and 22, for instance, varied more with such factors as the kind of district in which the men lived, or the atmosphere of the homes in which they were reared, or the measure of their native ability than with the circumstance that they had, or had not, been away on Service. Perhaps this can be shown most easily in tabular form. Table 26 shows (as a percentage) the amount of unemployment experienced in the course of 2 years by men who were away on Service and by men rejected as unfit in the light of these important 'background' factors.

It is clear that the weight of unemployment was less severe among those whose families lived in 'good' or 'fair' housing districts than among those whose families lived in 'poor' or 'slum' areas, and that this held true whether the men had been on Service or not. Indeed, the margin between those who lived in 'good' as compared with 'slum' districts was wider than the margin between those who had been on Service and those who had not, when men from similar types of district were compared.

Similarly, unemployment was less severe among those from 'good' homes than among those from homes classified as 'fair' or 'bad', and this held true whether the men had been on Service or not; but the margin between those who came from 'good' homes and those who came from 'poor' homes was wider than the margin between those who had been on Service and those who had not, when men from homes of similar quality were compared. A noteworthy feature was the heavy incidence of long-term unemployment among the men who came from 'poor' homes, whether they had been away on Service or rejected as unfit.

The unemployment experience of men of 'good' or 'average' scholastic ability was very similar, whether they had been on Service or not. The proportion of men of poor scholastic ability

TABLE 26

The proportion of men (as a percentage) who suffered unemployment between the ages of 20 and 22 in relation to certain social and environmental factors: men returned from National Service and men rejected as unfit for Service shown separately

	Rejected as unfit for Service			Completed 2 years National Service		
	Amount of unemployment (months in 2 years)			Amount of unemployment (months in 2 years)		
	0	*1–8*	*9+*	*0*	*1–8*	*9+*
Type of housing district						
Old, 'good' or 'fair' .	67	22·5	10·5 = 100	74	18·5	7·5 = 100
Old, 'poor' or 'slum'	52	22	26 = 100	55	25·5	19·5 = 100
'New' local-authority schemes . .	67	24	9 = 100	53	27	20 = 100
Home assessment						
'Good' . . .	64	23·5	12·5 = 100	69	19	12 = 100
'Fair' or 'Bad' .	56·5	21	22·5 = 100	46	30·5	23·5 = 100
Scholastic ability						
'A', 'B', 'C' (good or average) . .	68·5	21·5	10 = 100	68	18	14 = 100
'D', 'E' (poor) .	64·5	18·5	17 = 100	56·5	27	16·5 = 100

who wholly escaped unemployment during the 2 years was higher among the men rejected as unfit for Service, but the proportion with protracted unemployment was much the same in both groups. In general, when men of similar scholastic ability were compared, the gap was just as wide, in regard to unemployment experience, between those of 'good' or 'average' scholastic ability on the one hand and those of 'poor' ability on the other, as between those who had been on Service and those who had not.

In regard to each of these three background factors—type of housing district, quality of home, and level of scholastic ability

—the difference in unemployment experience between men fortunately placed at the good end of the social scale and those more poorly circumstanced tended to be wider among those who had been called up for Service than among those rejected as unfit, which suggests that absence on Service may have had a particularly unfortunate influence on the amount of subsequent unemployment among men of poorer social and environmental background.

10

The influence of social and environmental background on occupational status

The crippling effect of poor scholastic ability is reflected more clearly in the occupational status of the men, the kind of work in which they were employed, and especially so when occupational status at the age of 17 is compared with occupational status at the age of 22. Table 27 sets out the proportion of men employed in different types of work at these ages, showing separately the occupational status of men of 'good' or 'average' scholastic ability and men of 'poor' ability; and of men who had been away on National Service as compared with men rejected as unfit for Service.

In general, at the age of 17 the proportion of men in skilled manual work (as apprentices in course of training) and in semi-skilled work was appreciably higher among men subsequently called up for Service than among men subsequently rejected as unfit for Service, irrespective of the level of scholastic ability. But at the age of 22, 2 years after the completion of National Service in the case of those who had been called up, the position was different. Then, of men of 'average' or 'above average' scholastic ability the proportion employed in skilled and semi-skilled manual work was just about as high among those who had been rejected as among those called up for National Service. The group that had been on Service had lost many of its men from skilled manual work, whereas the group rejected as unfit for National Service had been able to keep its potentially skilled men in skilled manual work. Further, in this group of 'average' or 'above average' ability, among those who had been rejected as unfit the proportion of men in semi-skilled work was much higher at the age of 22 than it had been at the age of 17, whereas among those called up for Service the increase in the proportion of semi-skilled workers over the period was comparatively small. On the other hand there was, between the ages of 17 and 22, among those who had been away on Service a formidable increase in the proportion of men who were working as unskilled

TABLE 27

The proportion (as a percentage) of men in each type of occupation at age 17 and at age 22: men who had been on Service and men rejected as unfit, and men of 'good' or 'average' scholastic ability and men of 'poor' scholastic ability, shown separately

	At age 17		At age 22	
Nature of employment	*Completed 2 years Service*	*Rejected as unfit for Service*	*Completed 2 years Service*	*Rejected as unfit for Service*
Scholastic ability 'A', 'B', or 'C'				
(*good or average*)	(180)	(99)	(181)	(99)
Skilled manual . .	42	23	24	23
Semi-skilled . .	23	10	27	28
Unskilled manual .	9	40	23	33
Non-manual . .	25·5	27	24	12
Unemployed . .	0·5	..	2	4
	100	100	100	100
Scholastic ability 'D' or 'E'				
(*poor*)	(131)	(121)	(131)	(118)
Skilled manual . .	47	28	22	14
Semi-skilled . .	28	8	34	17
Unskilled manual .	16	36	34	50
Non-manual . .	9	27	10	12
Unemployed . .	..	1	..	7
	100	100	100	100

manual labourers, while during the same period the proportion in unskilled work actually fell among those who had been rejected as unfit for Service.

As was to be expected, men of 'poor' scholastic ability suffered more heavily than their brighter brothers in loss of occupational status between the ages of 17 and 22. Both the groups who had been on Service and those rejected as unfit lost many of their potentially skilled men, but the loss was rather heavier among those who had been away on Service; and the proportion in semi-skilled work showed a relatively greater increase over the 5 years among men who had been rejected as unfit than among men who had been away on Service. On the other hand, the proportion of men employed as unskilled manual labourers increased more rapidly over the period among those who had been away on Service than among those who had been rejected.

These findings assume added importance when viewed in the light of the earlier histories of the two groups, which had suggested that it would be unrealistic to expect the rejected lads to do as well in their subsequent careers as those who went on Service.

Other instances of the influence of basic social and environmental factors on the success of men in this age-group, as evidenced by occupational status at the age of 22, could equally well be quoted; among those who hailed from 'fair' or 'good' housing districts of older type, for example, the proportion of men in skilled manual work was well maintained between the ages of 17 and 22, but among those from 'poor' or 'slum' districts the loss of potential skill was much greater. Among those who had lived in 'new' local-authority housing areas, 21 per cent. of the lads subsequently rejected as unfit for Service had been in process of learning a skilled trade at the age of 17, and at the age of 22 this proportion was fully maintained; but among those who had been away on Service the proportion in skilled work had fallen from 34 per cent. at the age of 17 to 24 per cent. at the age of 22.

11

The decline in apprenticeship

Taking the study as a whole, the number of men who had been serving apprenticeships at the age of 17 was 163: at the age of 20 the number of skilled or potentially skilled men was 154, and at the age of 22 it had fallen to 119. The number in skilled manual work at the age of 22 was therefore about 73 per cent. of the number that had been in process of acquiring skill at the age of 17—74 per cent. among lads rejected as unfit for National Service, 72 per cent. among those called up for

Service—and the falling off between the ages of 20 and 22 was rather greater than among those who had been away on Service.

But these figures convey only an imperfect impression of the loss of potential skill which actually occurred, for they include men who commenced apprenticeships after the age of 17 and therefore tend to mask the loss of some who were apprentices at that age but subsequently fell through their apprenticeships. Of the 58 lads rejected as unfit for Service who were engaged in apprenticeships when they were 17 years of age only 37 were actually employed in skilled manual work at the age of 22 (64 per cent.); and of the 105 lads called up for Service who were in apprenticeships at the age of 17 only 60 (59 per cent.) were actually engaged in skilled manual work at the age of 22. This movement away from skill took place at all levels of scholastic ability, though it was most marked among those of 'poor' quality.

Only a small proportion of the lads who had expressed a desire for skilled manual work when they left school at the age of 14 were engaged in such work at the age of 22—25 per cent. of those rejected as unfit for National Service and 27 per cent. of those called up for Service. Of those who had wanted skilled work when they left school, between one-quarter and one-third were working as unskilled manual labourers at the age of 22. When groups of similar scholastic ability were compared, there was little difference between those called up for Service and those rejected as unfit in the proportion of men who had expressed a desire for skilled manual work who were in fact engaged in such work at the age of 22.

12

Leisure interests

The leisure interests of men in the 20 to 22 age-group had inevitably changed greatly from the interests of the same men at age 17, but it was disappointing that the proportion attending evening classes was only of the order of 3 or 4 per cent. There was no material difference between the leisure interests of those who had been on Service and those rejected as unfit for Service; only a handful of men in either group expressed themselves as being without leisure interests of some sort.

13

The incidence of crime

The incidence of crime affords one measure of social adaptation, and information is available about all the convictions recorded against the men included in this study between the ages of 8 and 22. Altogether, 54 of the 346 (15·6 per cent.) men called up for National Service, and 35 of the 222 (15·7 per cent.) men rejected as unfit for Service were convicted at least once between these ages. In each group about 12·2 per cent. of the men had been convicted at least once before reaching the age of 18 years, a figure very similar to that found in the original larger series from which the boys included in this study were drawn.[1] For obvious reasons, the incidence of delinquency among the lads who remained in civil life between the ages of 18 and 20 is scarcely comparable with that among the lads called up for National Service between these ages. Between the ages of 20 and 22 years, 14 of the 346 men called up (4·5 per cent.) were convicted at least once, 7 of them for the first time; during the same period 10 of the 222 rejected as unfit for Service (4·0 per cent.) were convicted at least once, 6 of them for the first time. The proportion of men convicted between the ages of 20 and 22 was, therefore, virtually the same among the men called up for Service and among those rejected as unfit for Service, and there was no material difference in the proportion of men who, having been convicted at least once between the ages of 14 and 18, had no further convictions between the ages of 20 and 22. The type of crime committed by men who had been called up did not differ from the type of crime committed by those who had been rejected as unfit for Service.

The incidence of crime was profoundly influenced by earlier social and environmental background, whether the men had been called up for Service or rejected as unfit. Among those who came from 'good' homes there was, in either event, much less crime than among those less happily placed. Those who lived in 'good' or 'fair' housing districts of pre-1914 construction had little more than half the amount of crime of those who hailed from 'poor' or 'slum' districts. The incidence of crime increased as the occupational status of the men declined. The

---

[1] *The Young Delinquent in His Social Setting*, op. cit.

volume of crime increased markedly as the volume of unemployment increased, whether the men had been on Service or not; and so on.

It was observed that with such basic environmental factors as the quality of the home and the type of district in which the men lived, as well as with scholastic ability, the difference in the proportions of men convicted between the good and the bad end of the scale tended to be wider among those who had been away on Service than among those who, having been rejected as unfit for National Service, had remained in civil life.

8

Epilogue

SUCH, then, is our picture of a group of Glasgow men in their early twenties, some of whom had completed their period of National Service while some, rejected as unfit for Service, had remained in civil life. It is not altogether a true picture of young men of that age in the city, for those whom it embraced had left school at the earliest permitted age; some had interrupted or thrown up apprenticeships to go on Service at the age of 18 instead of seeking deferment until their apprenticeship was completed, and some of those rejected as unfit for Service suffered not only from poor physique but also from that lost schooling born of previous illness which is such a serious matter for the physically handicapped. Yet the picture is true enough of the groups with which it deals, and they constitute a large part of the youth of the city.

It is a picture of conditions in a time of 'full employment'; yet 11 per cent. of the men were unemployed for 3 months or more in the course of the 2 years covered by the study: some worked but little during the period. Less than one man in every four was in skilled employment at the age of 22; one in three was an unskilled labourer. The housing conditions of the men had improved greatly during the 8 years since they left school, but even at the age of 22 one in every five still lived in a slum or near-slum area. Nearly all the men had some leisure interest, but only 3 or 4 per cent. were attending evening classes for further education. More than 15 per cent. of these men had been convicted at least once between the ages of 8 and 22; fully 4 per cent. were convicted between the ages of 20 and 22, just over half of them for the first time.

The national figures show a lower proportion of rejections for National Service on medical grounds than that experienced in our Glasgow study. The Glasgow boys were, on average, shorter and lighter than other National Servicemen when they were called up. Their gain in weight while on Service was substantial, but it left the boys in the study still in relatively the same position on release from Service as a control group.

The situation of the men who had been away on National Service inevitably invites comparison with that of the men who were rejected as unfit for Service and remained in civil life. The comparison is not an easy one to make, for in their early days the lads who subsequently went on Service had, as a group, social and environmental advantages which were bound to load the dice in their favour, apart from the question of National Service. There can be little doubt that Service helped some of the lads who were away; equally certainly it harmed others. But making due allowance for differences in social background, we are satisfied that, in the absence of complicating illness, the men rejected as unfit for Service experienced less unemployment and relatively fewer of them declined in occupational status between the ages of 20 and 22 than among those who had been on Service. Twenty-one per cent. of the men who had been away experienced difficulty in settling back into civil life, and although not all of these difficulties were of very serious or lasting import, they have to be kept in mind in seeking to assess the impact of Service. There was little difference between men who had been on Service and those who had not in the proportion convicted in the courts between the ages of 20 and 22; and there was no material difference between the groups in the proportion of men who, having been convicted at least once between the ages of 14 and 18, had no further convictions between the ages of 20 and 22.

One of the disquieting features of this study is the loss of potential skill that has been seen to take place between the ages of 17 and 22, among both those called up for Service and those rejected as unfit. Of those who had been serving apprenticeships at the age of 17, only 64 per cent. were in skilled work at the age of 22 among those rejected as unfit for Service, and only 59 per cent. among those who had been called up, though from their initial advantages much better results might have been expected from the latter group. Doubtless some of those who fell by the way scarcely had it in them to become good tradesmen, but the loss is too great; it must be a bad thing for the lads concerned and, in the long run, for the country. Surely, this trend towards loss of skill has not become a necessary feature of our social or industrial order? There can be little doubt that National Service is one factor contributing to the loss. The Service view on the matter is quite plain and understandable: it wants the men for Service purposes and is not much concerned with their trade advancement. An Army spokesman, Major-General V. D. G. Campbell, has summarized the matter by saying that 'the vast majority of young men going into the Army would be well advised to forget completely for the two years of their National Service anything to do with their civilian training and put all they could into their jobs as Officers, N.C.O.s, or soldiers; at the end of their Service they would find themselves far better fitted to compete successfully in civil life'.[1] It is not altogether surprising that this point of view does not always appeal to the young Serviceman or his parents. Perhaps the best answer would be to do more to encourage all apprentices to apply for deferment of their National Service until the completion of apprenticeship; doubtless even then some would drift away from their trade. In our experience, the drift away from training is largely due to realization by the lads that more and easier money can often be made in unskilled or semi-skilled jobs, that there are plenty of jobs of the sort available during a period of full employment, and that these jobs are free from the discipline of learning or the responsibilities that often go with skill. Surely, it would be well worth while to take lots of trouble to counteract that attitude of mind.

While, in the main, the influence of National Service has been unsettling, we have to record our conviction that its contribution to unsatisfactory performance is surpassed by the influence of the bad social and environmental conditions in which many of the lads in our study were reared. The after-effects of Service are apt to be more severe among those of poorest background. There is still urgent need for the improvement of living conditions, and, given better conditions, a need to inculcate something of the art of living.

[1] Report of conference on industry and National Service, Glasgow, 1 June 1955; *Scotsman*, 2 June 1955.

APPENDIX

Lads whose Period of National Service was not of 2 Years' Duration

THIRTY-ONE of the lads who volunteered, or were called up, for Service have been excluded from the main body of this report because their Service did not last for the ordinary period of 2 years; in one case (a Navy man) Service was extended beyond that period, and in the other 30 it fell short of it, almost invariably because the Serviceman was invalided out on medical grounds.

The duration of Service in these 30 cases is set out below:

Less than 3 months	11
3 months	3
6 ,, ...	6
12 ,, ...	3
18 ,, ...	7

Three of the 31 men thus excluded from the main study served overseas for some part of the time. The nature of their Service duties was described by the men as essentially 'military' in 19 cases, as 'trade' in none, and as 'other' in 9; in 3 (where Service had been of very short duration) the nature of duties was not stated. None of the men achieved promotion while on Service: one received some training in his trade, but this training did not count towards a civilian apprenticeship.

When seen in their own homes at the beginning of this study, 15 of the men said they had liked their period of Service, 11 said they had disliked it; 3 were neutral on the subject; 2 (who both served less than a fortnight) expressed no opinion.

Three of the 31 men returned to civilian employment immediately on discharge from the Forces, 11 took up civilian work after periods ranging up to 4 weeks, 11 after gaps of 1 to 3 months; and the remaining 6 after intervals of more than 3 months' duration.

Thirteen of the men returned to their pre-Service job, 7 to complete an apprenticeship or period of training; 16 took up other work, while 2 were for long unemployed. Twelve returned to work with their pre-Service employer.

In their first post-Service jobs 5 of the men earned less than 80s. a week; 15 received wages between 80s. and 119s. a week; 6 between 120s. and 159s.; 2 of the men were long unemployed; and the wages of three others were not stated.

When they were seen in their own homes at the age of 20,

    8 were serving apprenticeships or undergoing periods of training;

    3, having completed apprenticeships or periods of training, were employed as tradesmen in skilled manual work;

    4 were in semi-skilled manual work;

    8 were in unskilled manual work;

    2 were engaged in non-manual work; and

    5 were unemployed.

The nature of the employment of one man was not stated.

When the men were 22 years of age, at the end of the study, the employment picture was as follows:

    3 were still serving apprenticeships or undergoing periods of training;

    5, having completed apprenticeships or periods of training, were employed as tradesmen in skilled manual work;

    7 were engaged in semi-skilled manual work;

    10 were unskilled manual workers;

    3 were in non-manual work; and

    3 were unemployed.

The gross weekly wages received by the men at the ages of 20 and 22 are set out below:

	At age 20	At age 22
Less than 80s. . . .	4	0
80s.	9	1
120s.	10	17
160s.	1	5
200s.+	0	1
Unemployed	6	3
Not stated	1	4
	31	31

Many of the men changed jobs frequently in the course of the 2 years: frequency of change of job among them was greater than among the series of men who had completed 2 years' Service or among those who had been rejected as unfit for Service.

Many of the men experienced a good deal of unemployment.

In the course of the 2 years of the study 14 lost no working time through unemployment; one lost less than 4 weeks; 4 lost from 4 to 8 weeks; one lost from 9 to 12 weeks; and 11 lost more than 3 months. These figures were appreciably worse than those for the two groups of men described in the body of the report.

Seventeen of the men lost no working time on account of illness in the course of the 2 years between the ages of 20 and 22; 4 lost less than 4 weeks each; 4 lost from 4 to 8 weeks; 3 lost from 9 to 12 weeks; and 3 lost more than 3 months. These figures correspond fairly closely with the working time lost through illness over the same period by the men—described in the body of this report—who had been medically rejected as unfit for National Service.

At the beginning of this study, when the men were 20 years of age, 4 of the 31 were married; at the end, when they were 22 years of age, 10 were married.

Cumulative number of job changes	*After 6 months*	*After 12 months*	*After 18 months*	*After 24 months*
None . . .	16	10	10	8
One . . .	7	9	6	6
Two . . .	4	5	6	4
Three . . .	3	4	2	4
Four . . .	1	3	5	5
Five . . .	..	..	1	2
Not stated . .	..	..	1	2
	31	31	31	31

After their return from Service 3 of the 31 men were members of an organized social group.

When the available information about the background of these 31 lads was compared with that for the men who duly completed their 2-year period of National Service in the Army, it was found that among those invalided out of the Services the proportion who had been below average height at the time of leaving school was relatively high, as was the proportion classified at that time as being of poor physique. But in the personality assessment made by their school teachers when the lads left school those who were later invalided out of the Services made a better showing than the lads who completed 2 years' Service in the Army, and their level of scholastic ability was rather higher; for instance, 35 per cent. of them were placed in categories 'D' or 'E' (the two lowest) on scholastic assessment, as compared with 46 per cent. of those who completed 2 years' Service in the Army.

The general level of family assessment, as made by an experienced social worker, was rather higher among the boys who were invalided out than among those who completed 2 years' Service in the Army, but there was little difference between the two groups in the kind of housing district in which the lads lived or the severity of overcrowding prevailing in their homes.

The boys subsequently invalided out were, in the main, the sons of fathers on a rather lower level in the occupational scale than were the lads who completed their 2 years' period of Army Service; and, when their job-preference was ascertained at the time of leaving school, the boys subsequently invalided out did not so often seek skilled work. This was borne out by later experience; for at the age of 17 a lower proportion of these lads was engaged in skilled manual work and there were fewer apprentices among them. As a group, they had lost more working time between the ages of 14 and 17 than had the lads who completed their 2 years' Army Service. Many had remained in the same job throughout that period, but a relatively high proportion had changed jobs four or more times in the course of the 3 years—29 per cent. as against 17 per cent. of those who completed 2 years' Army Service. Further, at the age of 17, a higher proportion of those who were later invalided out of the Services still regarded themselves as unsettled in their jobs; 50 per cent. of them still regarded their jobs as merely stop-gap, as compared with 30 per cent. of the lads who completed 2 years' Army Service.

INDEX

PRINTED IN
GREAT BRITAIN
AT THE
UNIVERSITY PRESS
OXFORD
BY
CHARLES BATEY
PRINTER
TO THE
UNIVERSITY